LISTEN, HANS

LISTEN, HANS

BY

DOROTHY THOMPSON

HOUGHTON MIFFLIN COMPANY · BOSTON

The Riverside Press Cambridge

THE GENESIS OF THIS BOOK

THE BROADCASTS in this volume were addressed every Friday, between March and September, 1942, to a friend in Germany. They were transmitted over the short-wave facilities of the Columbia Broadcasting System, as part of their program to Europe. They were passed by the Coordinator of Information, afterward the Office of War Information. But they were not composed in collaboration with any government agency, being an individual and private effort, announced as such by the C.B.S. in every introduction.

They are, as they pretend to be, specifically addressed to one person. This person exists. He is an old friend, and a man whose mind is thoroughly familiar to me.

In choosing to address myself to him in a deeply personal manner, I was, of course, aware that my words would be heard by anyone who could listen. And I have thought of them, too.

But the advantage to me in speaking to 'Hans' (whose name, of course, is not Hans — or is it?) is that it compelled me to enter into *his* mind, to reconstruct what I knew *he* has thought, to develop what clues I have received as to what *he* is thinking now, as the war unrolls.

Hans is a not unrepresentative German, of a certain class and type. His thinking is not unique. He is a German patriot and he is not a Nazi. Previous to the war our basic thinking on European and world affairs was harmonious. That line of thought was not confined to Hans and to me. Thousands and thousands of other Germans, of his generation and mine, thought the same way. I can presume that his basic thinking has not changed — as mine has not. I have evidence that it has not changed. Therefore, through him, I have sought to re-establish contact with men and women of like mind in an enemy country.

Now, the question is in order: May any private citizen set out to establish contacts with old friends in enemy countries? I should hope not. For the only logical procedure is that there should be a clear and established policy of our Administration regarding the principles, tone, and strategy of psychological warfare.

Before I started with these broadcasts, I attempted to get a clear line on what our policy was. But it is clear that our policy is not yet established, but in the process of developing.

The status was (and as I write these words still is) the following:

The broadcasting stations were then under private initiative. They planned and carried out their own programs with the advice and consent of the Office of War Information and the Office of Inter-American Relations. There was then no complete integration of the whole effort. There were no basic statements about policy beyond the Atlantic Charter, which has never been interpreted. Thus, whoever went on the air had to find out by trial and error whether he was doing the right thing.

Yet, these broadcasts were not a hobby. They were impelled by a deep conviction that politics was a prime instrument of the war. It seemed to me to be an area in which I could be of use. For I have spent more than twenty years of my life trying to understand the mind of Germany and studying the mental and social shape of Europe, and it seemed to me that now, in this war, that knowledge, and the intuitions born of long observation, might be of use.

Therefore, I did not consider such broadcasts as these as an individual enterprise, but in conference with the officials of the C.B.S. suggested a cooperative program, designed to touch various circles in Germany. Of the suggestions made, the C.B.S. accepted five, and these five, which again are only segments of the whole plan and of the C.B.S. and Office of War Information effort, have been worked out cooperatively.

C.B.S. chose, as part of a common program, two theologians, both of them eminent: Paul Tillich, a German Protestant, now an American citizen, and Professor of Theology at the Union Theological Seminary of New York, whose weekly sermons to the German people are, in my mind, among the classic documents of this war; Professor Dietrich von Hildebrand, formerly Professor at the University of Vienna, now Professor at Fordham University, who collaborated for this purpose with a group of young Catholics in this country, and is one of the signers of the great Catholic 'Manifesto on the War' published late in August in the liberal Catholic Weekly *The Commonweal*; Max Werner, author of *The Battle of the World* and *The Great Offensive*, military scientist and expert on Russia, whose broadcasts have been repeatedly and violently attacked by Doctor Goebbels — our most gratifying praise; and Horst von Baerensprung, formerly the vigorously anti-Nazi police commissioner of the city of Magdeburg, then for many years adviser of the League of Nations to the Chinese Government, and expert on the Far East.

It was my desire to embody samples of all these broadcasts in this volume, and it was only my publisher's apprehension that the result would be too voluminous and confusing that prevented it.

As editor to all of us, we have had the services of Hermann Budzislawski, who got in Hitler's hair for years, as editor of the intransigently democratic and trenchantly critical *Weltbuehne*.

All of these men have served as volunteers, giving great amounts of their time to helping fight the democratic war of ideas. It has been an immense pleasure to me to work with them, because we share to such a great extent the same view of the issues of the war as they must appear in Europe, and a similar belief in what is the correct approach.

In the months in which we have worked, we have found nothing but the most courteous collaboration from the officials of the Columbia Broadcasting System and have been allowed almost complete freedom by the Office of War Information. I wish to thank them both for allowing this publication. As for the style of these broadcasts, they were sometimes written in German, and always *thought* in German, and must therefore be regarded as translations.

CONTENTS

PART ONE
THE INVASION OF THE GERMAN MIND

I

ON PSYCHOLOGICAL WARFARE

PSYCHOLOGICAL WARFARE is an assault on the mind and the emotions of the enemy. The first prerequisite, therefore, is to understand that mind. The strategy in political or psychological warfare does not differ profoundly from military strategy. Every good general tries to understand the plans of the enemy; that is, what is in his mind. For only by understanding what is in his mind can he circumvent those plans. He approaches that understanding with coolness and objectivity — not hatred. He can even be fascinated and impressed by what he learns. But he learns in order to turn back the enemy's plans upon himself, and so frustrate him.

If this is true for generals conducting a military campaign, it is even more necessary for those conducting a campaign of political warfare. One major reason for the setbacks of the war in its initial and political stages — in the stages of the 'bloodless victories' of Hitler — was failure on the part of the leaders of Britain and France to understand either the nature of National Socialism or the mentality that produced National Socialism and accepted Hitler's leadership.

That mentality cannot be assailed from without, but only from within, and only with the ideas that are already present in the enemy's mind. The object of political warfare is to secure the collaboration of the enemy's forces for his defeat, or realign the forces in such a way as to turn a hostile nation into a friend.

Therefore, the first axiom of political warfare is: Know your enemy. Reach him by playing upon his own mentality. His mind is like a defense in depth. Before one can assault it, one must have surveyed the entire terrain; one must know where his fortresses are strong, and where they are weak; where they can be penetrated, and where there will be terrific resistance.

This raises the question: Is there such a thing as the 'German Mind'?

Our emphasis on individualism and economic forces has led us to doubt whether there is such a thing as a national 'mind form.' We tend to think of nations as agglomerations of many different mentalities or as purely economic groupings, or we pick out what seems to be a leading characteristic of a people and play upon that alone, disregarding other conscious or unconscious psychological factors. Unfortunately, far too few studies have been made of the mentality of peoples; we know more about the anthropologies of peoples than about their psychologies.

Yet, there are distinguishable national mentalities. That all the people in any nation seldom react unanimously at the same time and in the same way to any suggestion does not prove the absence of definite tendencies. Neither does the fact that apparently all think alike at any moment in history indicate that that common action is universally or permanently 'typical.'

In any case it is the common mind form that distinguishes a nation or a culture, and not anthropological characteristics.

But what are the clues to the mind of a people?

The clues lie in the history, geography, social structure, and culture of a nation — its philosophy and art. These are the factors that influence or determine its national psychology and its behavior. It is futile to try to understand a people merely by observing how they are behaving in any one moment of their history. A description of their contemporary behavior is not an explanation of it. The explanation lies much farther back and deeper down.

And of all the factors counted, history is probably the most powerful. For a nation's history is its most universal social inheritance.

Every member of each nation has been subjected, consciously and unconsciously, to certain common historical influences transmitted to him by fact and myth in the most impressionable years of his life. Therefore, the history of a people, and the way that people has, from time to time, interpreted that history to itself, reveal to us a pattern of historical behavior. From history we learn how a nation has behaved under the various circumstances of its life, and this knowledge gives us a partial picture, at least, of the national personality.

History may reveal cleavages in the national mentality, especially when considered in relation to the culture and social structure. There may be an aristocracy who live in a quite different cultural climate from that of the middle class or workers. It may even live in a different historical climate, since it may have had a different social history.

What can we find out about the German mind from a study of German history?

II

ON GERMAN HISTORY

THE FIRST THING that strikes the eye in exploring the terrain of German history is that it is characterized, not by its continuity, but by its episodic character. It reveals, not unity, but disunity; not conformity, but contradictions. The history of Germany is the history of a people who became a national state centuries after Britain and France had found their characteristic national forms. It became partially unified — but not completely — only seventy-odd years ago, and then the German nation-state did not include the whole of the Germanic peoples, even those organized and living as 'Germans.' That part of the German people unified in the Reich have lived one common national and cultural life for less than half the length of history of the American Constitution. Germany is that nation of Europe with least uniformity and continuity in its history.

'THE FIRST REICH'

Germans count three 'Reichs' since Charlemagne. The Empire of Charlemagne was not German in any national sense. It included France, the Low Countries, and large parts of eastern and southern Europe, and broke to pieces immediately after the death of its founder.

The Middle Ages were filled with the fiction of a 'First German Reich' called 'The Holy Roman Empire of German Nationality.' For centuries it was unclear whether the real governor of this 'Reich' was the Pope, or the Emperor and dynasty whose German nationality was the sole reason for calling the Reich 'German.' Actually the Holy Roman Empire furnished the roof for innumerable dynastic and ecclesiastical governing bodies, resting on no popular or national foundations at all, and waging war with each other continually.

In the course of centuries this Reich underwent profound changes; the nations of continental Europe began to take form, and the final blow to the whole system was dealt by Napoleon.

THE BEGINNINGS OF 'THE SECOND REICH'

What was left of it at the beginning of the nineteenth century was the so-called 'Bund' of Germanic and non-Germanic states; those in the Austro-Hungarian monarchy; the petty states of German princes; and over against these the rising and powerful military state of Prussia. There was still no 'Germany,' in a unified national sense. And the leader of the Bund was the Emperor of Austria — who was, at the same time, the head of such non-Germanic states as Hungary and Bohemia, the governor of parts of Italy, and the inheritor of portions of the dissolving Ottoman Empire.

After Napoleon's defeat, the rest of the nineteenth century was given over to the building of some kind of German state. The middle of the century — the thirties and forties — saw a great popular national wave, following the French example, sweep Europe, and for a time it seemed as though the Second German Reich would be created as part of this national and revolutionary movement — the one that saw the rise of Mazzini and Garibaldi in Italy.

But the German Revolution of 1848, hailed by the great Italian liberators and warmly supported by such poets as Walt Whitman, did not succeed. It was suppressed, and suppressed in a manner which strongly recalls the fate of the Weimar Republic, between 1918 and 1933. Actually the 1848 Revolution succeeded in getting the power. But it had no *sense* of power, and yielded it to the aristocratic Junker class and the armies of the King. It gave up power when threatened by force.

If one jumps nearly a century, to 1932, one finds a parallel. The Prussian Minister of the Interior in the German Republic, when asked by Franz von Papen, Reichschancellor and way-paver for Hitler, to dissolve the Social Democratic Prussian Government and give over the control of one hundred thousand armed Prussian police, did so 'rather than spill a drop of blood.'

Thus history repeated itself, for almost exactly the same thing had happened in 1849, when the revolutionaries in Berlin, who *had* the power, and who represented, as did the

German Republic, an attempt to integrate German nationalism with the trends of the national revolutions in the rest of
Europe, yielded to the King's armies under General
Wrangel. 'We will bow only to force,' said the 1848 revolutionaries. 'Then bow,' said General Wrangel. 'I am it.'

*'The Second German Reich' was not, therefore, the creation of a
popular revolutionary movement, in harmony with other European
movements of the times. It was the creation of an aristocratic Prussian military caste.* Not the 1848 popular revolution, but Bismarck's Reich of Blood and Iron created it.

The revolution that *wished* to create it, and that produced
the German *Marseillaise, Deutschland ueber Alles*, had been
shoved aside.

(*Deutschland ueber Alles* is not a song glorifying conquest
and claiming the world for Germans. It is a song glorifying
the idea of country over king.)

'THE SECOND REICH'

The New Germany was created between 1864 and 1870
by the Prussian Army, and always thereafter bore the characteristics of that fact. To understand the meaning of this,
let us imagine that the United States had not been created
by the Constitutional Congress, but by the armies of General Washington with the new state an extension of those
armies. And let us suppose that those armies had been
formed by making the great plantation-owners into officers,
and drafting their slaves to serve under them.

That is how Friedrich Wilhelm I created his armies: he made the landowners into officers and drafted their serfs as their soldiers.

The new German state, therefore, 'The Second Reich,' under the leadership of military Prussia was both an instrument of war — it was created in the course of three wars — and a social instrument for preserving the interests of the Prussian estate-owning and military caste.

And this Second German Reich of Bismarck's was still not national in any conclusive sense.   It was for what was called 'The Small German Solution.'

After fighting a war against Denmark in alliance with Austria, it fought a war against Austria for the purpose of taking the leadership of the Bund away from Austria, and throwing her out of it, to lead a life of her own with the non-Germanic states around her — exactly the reverse of what Hitler did seventy years later.

The war of 1870 against France was for the purpose of annexing Lorraine, thereby extending the German frontier beyond the Rhine, and weakening the new state's strongest neighbor.

Bismarck did not want Lorraine, but his chauvinists forced him to it.

But 'The Second Reich,' with Prussia sovereign in it, and the Prussian military caste dominating it, *was still not an integrated national German state*. It had for the first time in 1866 a customs union. But it had no common political structure throughout its whole history. Saxony and Bavaria, Hesse, Baden, and many other German states still had their own princes and complete autonomy. There was immense sectionalism, with the southern German states perennially leaning toward the Austro-Hungarian complex, a fact upon which Allied propaganda played in the last war.

French politics attempted the same overtures in this war, and even in French concentration camps Rhineland Germans were separated from the others, as being easier to influence.

THE INTERIM OF THE REPUBLIC

This Second German Reich suffered disaster in 1918, but not a disaster sufficient to uproot the tradition of its foundation. The Weimar Republic was, in its origins, a strange phenomenon. It was also, in a perverted sense, a creation of the German Army — strictly an interim creation. For the Army put up the Republican leaders as a fence for its own defeat. It was the Army which sent Kaiser Wilhelm II into exile.

The Allies accepted the liberal front, and it was the German Republic and not the German military leaders who signed the Treaty of Versailles — an historic and psychological mistake of the first importance.

It was liberal Germany — heir of 1848, briefly recognized by the ruling caste for opportunist reasons, the Germany that wanted to collaborate as an equal with the

western powers — who was thus burdened with the unpopular document. And the ink was not dry upon it before
the same military caste who had created the Second Reich
was busy plotting to 'come back,' enormously aided in their
conspiracy by the stupidity of the Allies.

*Yet the Weimar Republic created the first integrated German
national state.*

By removing the dynasties that had vested interests in
many Germanies rather than in one Germany, it went far
on the way to making a really integrated German nation,
and it tried its powerless best to include German Austria in
the nation. The pro-western Social Democrats were as
strongly for the *Anschluss* with Austria as was Hitler later.
And the very first paragraph in the constitution of democratic post-war Austria, which made Austria for the first
time an exclusively German state, reads: 'Austria is an integral part of the German Reich.'

'THE THIRD REICH'

The Third Reich is the Reich of Hitler. And in some
respects the work of building it was prepared by the Republic. A German nation came into being, uniform throughout
all its parts, centralized under a single political leadership,
and including all the genuine and sizeable Germanic
groups: the German Austrians; the Germans of old Bohemia; and, by arrangement with Mussolini and transfers of
population, the Germans of the Southern Tirol.

Now, it was extremely difficult not to be convinced by Hitler's demand for the creation of a *Volksstaat*; a popular and inclusive German nation.

For the movement for Germanic union goes right back to European revolutionary trends of a deeply popular nature. The revolutions of 1848 and 1918, neither of them anti-European or anti-democratic, but, on the contrary, movements deeply allied with European and democratic thought and tendencies, had both wanted such a union. Hitler could even call on the ideas of Woodrow Wilson, idol of the young Slavic nations, to support him in this. Actually he could invoke 1848 or Wilson more justly than Bismarck and the Prussian Junkertum, for they had always wanted 'their' Germany rather than 'Germany.'

Had Hitler confined himself to the ideal of Germanic union, inside the European framework of nations and in harmony with European trends of the last century, he would have been on extremely strong ground, not only internally, but externally as well.

The great weakness of French and British leadership which led them to Munich was that they hoped, even if not wholly convinced, that this *was* his framework, and thus sustained him on a false premise.

In order to 'form a more perfect union' of Germany as a European nation-state inside the framework of other European nation-states, Hitler would have had to choose, once and for all, between the various and conflicting tendencies of German history. He would have had to reject both the First Reich and the Second Reich, and reject them definitely. He would have had to bring the Revolution of 1848 at last into full reality and power.

To create a German nation-state in the framework of the nations of Europe, he would have had to define, once and for all, the political frontiers of such a state. For defined political frontiers are the essence of a nation-state.

It looked for a moment as though he intended to do this, and as though the makers of Munich had not conceded in vain. That was when he made the categorical statement: 'The Sudetenland represents my last territorial demand in Europe.'

He did not mean it, as events very shortly demonstrated.

But again a German and European tragedy of the first importance had occurred. Again a Germany that was almost completely in harmony with the main currents of European thought had tried to do the popular thing and failed, this time because of the blindness of the rest of Europe and the isolationism of America.

The German Republic had tried by diplomatic means, for instance, to get union with German-Austria, when the *Anschluss* idea was exactly as popular, or more so, in both countries as it was under Hitler. But the German Republic could not even get a customs union. Had the German Republic really been able to consolidate the Reich, it would have appeared in the German mind as 'the Liberator' and

Hitler might never have got beyond his beer hall. I say he *might* not, for there were many things in the German mind that might have coughed him up, anyhow.

For, fearful of its neighbors, fearful of internal disorders, and mediocre in leadership, the Weimar Republic repeated the fault of the 1848 revolutionaries, and *never got an army loyal to it*. The Reichswehr, to be sure, was drastically reduced by the treaties, but it remained intact and aloof, biding its time. It bided its time until defeat, inflation, and depression had all done their work, and then backed Hitler. Hitler began his political life as a Reichswehr propagandist and agent. That the Reichswehr and a few powerful industrialists interested in rearmament and fearful of communism should have backed a waif out of a Vienna flophouse by way of the trenches, with an enormous appeal over desperate middle-class masses, was merely evidence of their unexhausted sense of power and great political shrewdness. To get a popular demagogue to seduce the masses in the interest of their suppressors is a formula as old as politics. It has been described by Aristotle and recommended by Machiavelli. Thus, again, Germany moved toward greater unity, not by a genuine popular movement in harmony with the rest of the nations of Europe, but through a conspiracy of military power.

Yet this time the result was different. If the Third Reich has turned out to be more powerful than even Bismarck's Second Reich, it is also more amorphous. For Hitler turned out to be, not the instrument of the Prussian military caste alone, but the expression of the whole unconscious mind and history of the German nation. *And in that mind, expressed through Hitler, are all the confusions of German history — the confusions which are the menace of Europe and the world and which grow directly out of German historical indigestion.*

What is Germany?

On this question the German nation as a whole has never to this day made up its mind!

Is Germany a mythological and mystic realm, like the Holy Roman Empire, the 'First Reich,' embracing undefined areas and holding them together by an idea?

Is Germany Germanic and non-Germanic peoples together, dominated, as was the old Austro-Hungarian monarchy, by Germanic sovereignty?

Is Germany a state which is the General Headquarters and instrument of a Prussian military caste, ruling its own people and conquering others by blood and iron?

Is Germany a modern national state, resting on popular foundations, and living in a Europe of similar national states, perhaps *prima inter pares,* but still on a basis of equality?

In German history it has been *every one of these things.*

To ask a German, therefore, 'What is the *true* Germany?' is to ask a question which cannot be answered historically, but only by desire or by a shrug. All of them have, at one time or another, *been* 'the true' Germany to the Germans who lived under them.

In the German mind, therefore, is every cleavage of European history, and these cleavages have never yet been resolved. This is evident in German literature past and contemporary. It is full of morbid self-analysis, a recurrent posing of the question: What does it mean to be a German? The question would seem preposterous for an Englishman, a Frenchman, an American, or even a Pole after centuries of subjection, to ask of himself.

If cleavages are not resolved by decisions — decisions to take this course or that, a nation, like a person, suffers from schizophrenia. A nation, unable to make a choice, resolves its cleavages into mystic confusion and outward violence.

The National Socialist Third Reich has *not* resolved and clarified the historic confusions of the German mind. On the contrary, it has conjoined *all* the cleavages, and taken into itself all the dilemmas.

The Third Reich is attempting a synthesis of all the Germanies of history, and is able to synthesize them in only one common characteristic: Expansionism.

In the First mystic 'German' Reich of the Middle Ages, no European asked of another, Are you a Frenchman, or a German, or an Italian? He asked, 'Are you a Christian?' The European owed his ultimate allegiance in that Reich to a church and to a Germanic emperor — a Germanic emperor without a German nation.

In Naziism there is an enormous recrudescence of this historic memory, in weird perverted, modern form. Again a cross is to fly over all Europe — perhaps over the whole world — but it is to be the hooked cross of German dynamism: the new religion of Naziism. The question is newly put, not: Are you a Frenchman, an Italian? But: Are you a Nazi?

Thus, non-Germans, as once before in history, can enter into the Reich by way of a cross and a creed.

Yet this time sovereignty over this realm is conceived of as exercised by a nation, not an emperor, with the Leader merely the instrument of the nation. Not the Emperor, ruling by divine right, but the 'Master Folk,' ruling by natural right, through a 'Folk' Leader.

At the same time, however, the German nation is to remain intact, as a distinct and free nation-state, in a Europe where there are no more free nations and sovereign states.

And, finally, this nation-state is to rest on and be ruled by a military caste of officers and administrators.

Thus has Hitler tried to synthesize in the Third Reich the ideas of the Holy Roman Empire, the Austro-Hungarian Empire, the Prussian caste-state, and the revolutionary concepts of 1848 and 1918.

But they can be synthesized only for purposes of war. No state at peace can manage to be all these things, for they are profoundly contradictory.

THE RESULTS OF HISTORICAL CONFUSION

Such a psychological confusion, in a nation as in an individual, induces a mental breakdown expressing itself in physical outbreaks. Schizophrenics are dangerous. Unable to make up their minds, they make up their wills. Unable to create their world, they imagine their world — and find reality against them. The Third Reich that is to last for a thousand years is the Reich that never was on land or sea. It is not even placed in *time*.

Naziism has one foot in the Middle Ages and one foot in the twenty-first century. It is nowhere in the present. It has not turned its back upon Charlemagne, or the Holy Roman Empire, or the Prussian military-caste state, or the Austrian idea of Germanic organization of the Slavs and other 'lesser breeds,' or the idea of the popularly founded nation. It is an enormous indigestion, vomiting fire and flame, and not even clearing its own stomach in the process.

Unable to break with its historic confusions and contradictions, the dominant characteristic of the German mind is morbid frustration and despair. This is admitted by one of the keenest modern analysts of German psychology, Professor Richard Mueller-Freienfels, who finds the German mind *tragic*. It *is* tragic. And so is Professor Mueller-Freienfels. For, in his book, *The German: His Psychology*, written in 1921 and re-edited in 1929, he concludes, optimistically:

> What about Germany's relationship to the rest of the world? Folk psychology, as we understand it, will grant, not only to the German nation, but also to every other nation, the right to live according to its own nature. If Ger-

many at any time had dreams of world domination (and such hopes have only been expressed by scattering, unrepresentative persons), then it is just the appreciation of national singularity that must aid us in working against such vain desires. The frightfully stupid expression to the effect that the whole world will in future be restored to health by the example of Germany must be cast into oblivion for all time. It is quite sufficient that we Germans be cured of our ills, by following our *real* example, that is, by growing to be a true expression of German nature.

But Professor Mueller-Freienfels, who regards Faust as the true folk-symbol and the only serene expression of German clarification, is today a Nazi. No doubt he can find some of Goethe in Naziism. For everything is in it, unresolved and undigested.

SOME CONCLUSIONS TO BE DRAWN

But even this very brief and shockingly condensed reconnaissance of the historic content of the German mind must lead us to one conclusion that should influence our political warfare:

The attempt further to confuse the German mind is wasteful and dangerous.

For a mind that can consume and rationalize such contradictions can consume and rationalize any number more. The German outburst is less the result of a clear and definite plan and choice than the eruption of a mentality *unable to make a choice*, and therefore resorting to a blind 'drive of the will.'

Our political warfare should seek to bring into full consciousness the contradictions in the German unconscious. It should seek to force the German mind to make itself up; and it should attempt to direct it, by the coldest common sense and reason, into that one of its conflicting directions which runs parallel to the direction of the rest of the world, and with the promise, founded in sincerity and logic, that this direction has a future.

GERMAN NATIONHOOD IS DESIRABLE

The unification of the German nation is *in harmony with, not in contradiction to,* all the tendencies of western civilization. It is in conflict with the idea of a mystic realm of cross and creed, and in conflict with the old Austro-Hungarian pan-German idea. The conflict of a unified Germany with the rest of western civilization arises out of the forces impelling the consolidation and the purposes to which it has been put, and out of the fact that it has not broken with previous Germanic history.

To suggest to Germany that she might be dismembered, an idea which despite the Atlantic Charter is rife among small nations and among the foreign offices of large ones, is to attack the fortress of the German mind in that spot where it is a veritable Verdun, and to destroy the only tendency with which we can eventually come to terms. For in the last hundred years, whether through the liberal revolutions of 1848 and 1918 or the reactionary periods of later

Prussianism and Hitlerism — through all the contradictions and confusions — the urge toward national unity is the sole consistent popular and democratic line.

Germans, who hate this war; who do not believe in the conquest of Europe or the conquest of the East, or in the Master Race, or in the Cross and Creed of the Nazi Party, do believe in Germanic unity as the one clear and positive European idea in the midst of antediluvian rubbish. And Germans who would gladly see Hitler perish and Europe live freely will fight to the last drop of blood for German unity. The fear of the dismemberment of Germany constitutes Hitler's greatest psychological asset today.[1]

FALSE ANALOGIES

The most dangerous idea with which certain persons in and out of foreign offices are playing is the idea of *securing permanent European peace* by German dismemberment.

The last war ended by destroying the Austro-Hungarian Empire and preserving, however weakened, the German nation-state. That was not very successful, so what is now being considered in some circles is just the opposite: restoring some form of the Austro-Hungarian Empire plus southern Germany, and dissolving the German national state.

[1] Theodore Kaufman's *Germany Must Perish*, touted by its publishers, Argyle Press, of Newark, as 'The Book Hitler Fears,' is, on the contrary, The Book Hitler Wants. It has been quoted and publicized inside Germany by Doctor Goebbels to prove to the German people that Hitler's war is veritably a war for the survival of Germany as a race and nation. It turned out to be, therefore, as any sensible person would have known, a piece of *Nazi* propaganda — Nazi in effect because invaluable to the Nazis.

But the dissolution of the Austro-Hungarian Empire was not accomplished by the military intervention of the Allies, but by revolt of subject nationalities within it, merely assisted by the Allies, largely in a political manner. Dissolution was implicit in the ramshackle and antedated structure. *No such dissolution is implicit in the German nation-state*. On the contrary, a hundred years of history show a steady movement in the opposite direction, and this movement is the only movement in German history which has not, until the birth of the Third Reich, been wholly expansionist and aggressive!

I repeat: The history of Germany, unlike the history of the Austro-Hungarian Empire, has been a history of coalescence, not of disintegration. It is, like the history of every nation of Europe, and like our own, a history of movement away from particularism toward national unity, and it cannot be too strongly emphasized that this movement is especially to be noted in every liberal epoch. The movement has never been furthered by aristocratic, dynastic, reactionary, or caste interests, but by the deepest popular trends in the German masses — exactly as similar movements were inspired in France, Italy, and the United States, *by the people*, not by the classes.

If it should be our purpose to underline and support those things in German historical development which tend to bring Germany into the framework of a popularly founded, democratically inspired European system, then we must support German unity.

DANGERS IN FOSTERING DISINTEGRATION

Furthermore, it is a fantastic illusion, of infinite foolishness, to believe that we can support disruptive, particularist, or reactionary forces in one country, even in a defeated enemy country, without those disruptive forces spreading to the next.

Can we not learn from the mistakes of our enemies? That is Hitler's Grand Illusion! He believes that he can destroy the nations of Europe without destroying Germany as a nation, and he is absolutely wrong. Many Germans know it. To try to put Hitlerism into reverse is to share its major error.

The particularist forces in Germany are reactionary and dynastic. They are without the slightest popular foundation. If diplomats believe they are representative, it is because diplomats seldom meet anyone except the 'best people,' and have been demonstrably more wrong about social forces in countries than almost any other observers.

If, in the modern world, we begin playing for a peace policy on the lines of Metternich and the Holy Alliance, we will one day find either a victorious Germany or Russia the arbiter of all Europe. And it will serve us right. For failure to comprehend the lessons of history is an unforgivable crime in statesmen.

We are fighting this war for the Four Freedoms, and I hope for a great many more than the four. Among them must surely be counted the freedom of peoples to determine

their own way of life, provided they grant the same right to
others. It is absolutely impossible to have one principle for
a friend, and another for an enemy, if principles are involved in the war at all. And unless principles are involved,
we have the bleak prospect of a world that will never come
to peace, for principles are the only foundation for possible
permanent agreement.

We have to stop thinking that any one nation, including our own, is the whole of society, at any time or in any
place. Nations are each of them a part of a larger society.
Culturally they are part of western civilization or oriental
civilization; economically, they are all part of a world
economy.

A disrupted Germany cannot be a democratic Germany.
To keep it disrupted, one will constantly have to suppress
all the democratic elements.

But an undemocratic Germany will poison all the areas
around it. One cannot maintain a democratic Poland or
Czechoslovakia in its neighborhood.

So it is fearfully shortsighted of some of the democratic
leaders of the smaller nations to be for German disruption.
They will not survive such a Germany.

We must also get out of our minds the idea that the
Austro-Hungarian Empire was not expansionist, whereas
the 'Prussian' state was. That idea is historical nonsense.

The Austro-Hungarian monarchy was expansionist to
the last breath of its doddering life. The First World War

was caused by the expansionism of this empire in the world of the Slavs, and actually can be dated from 1908 when Austria annexed Bosnia and brought the Germanic world up against Serbia and eventually Russia.

And the present war was precipitated by a pan-German Austrian. *Mein Kampf* is an Austrian manifesto even more than a German. In it Hitler espouses the pan-Germanism of the Austro-Hungarian Empire. He wished *Anschluss* with Austria, not in order to create a unified German national state, but in order to lay claim to the rôle of the old Austro-Hungarian Empire. This time he prepared to put the whole Germanic world in the service of that idea, and in the service of the Prussian idea as well, and at the same time.

And let us never forget that Hitler's first move outside Germanic territory was not in any area previously claimed by 'Germany,' but in the Slavic territory over which the Austro-Hungarian Empire had once ruled: Bohemia (Czechia).

We must stop making political judgments of world-wide importance on the basis of our likes and dislikes: that the Prussians are wicked and disagreeable and the Austrians nice — especially those highly cultivated Austrians whom most diplomats meet. When the Nazis invaded Austria, the Austrian population behaved with a savagery toward Jews and other minorities that put the Prussians in the shade. The historic fact is that the Austrian Empire was exactly as expansionist as the Prussian, though it preferred to use Reich Germans to fight for it, and to marry its way around rather than fight at all.

The one hope in stopping pan-Germanism is to insist on *national* Germanism, and the integration of the German nation as a strictly limited nation in a Europe of strictly limited nations.

Actually, it can be proved to the Germans — and our politics should concentrate on proving it — that they cannot merge the expansionist ideas of the non-national Austro-Hungarian Empire, plus the cross-and-creed idea of the Holy Roman Empire of the Nazi Party, plus the aggressive military caste state, and *keep the German nation.*

It can be proved in absolute logic, demonstrated by past history and by contemporary events, that victory for Hitler's amorphous aims would lead to the disintegration of the German nation, just as Austrian pan-Germanism led to the dissolution of the remnants of the Second Reich in the Austro-Hungarian Empire. The logic of national states is that they must live in a world of other national states. There is no such thing possible as one national-state sovereign in a Europe of disintegrated nations.

A slogan for this war ought to be: We have no quarrel with the German nation, *as a nation.* Stalin has been smart enough to see this and say it. We have a quarrel with Germano-Austrian pan-Germanism that wants again to lord it over subject peoples; we have a quarrel with the revival of mediaeval ideas of conquest by cross-and-creed fifth columns; we have a quarrel with the turning of Germany into a herd of neo-Teutonic Knights, out for loot. These should be the targets of our politics.

We should try consistently to lead Germany to a fourth embodiment in which the conflicts and contradictions of German history will be resolved in the only way they can be resolved.

The world is sick and tired of German wars that are apparently fought by Germany partly for the purpose of determining through them what the German destiny may be. The German mind is contradictory, despairing, and tragic, but we are all heartily sick of suffering with her. If the German mind cannot make itself up, then we must make it up for her, by force. If necessary we must keep it made up by force, long enough to establish it in certain directions.

But we should never despair of German aid in achieving that clarity. And we must select out of the mess of Germanic trends those that are basically compatible with our world.

It is not necessary to put anything into the German mind that is not in it already. It is extremely necessary to purge it of certain ideas and aid Germany to canalize the others in directions which can be integrated with the rest of the world.

No good general attacks on all points of a line — points weak and strong — at the same time. He attacks the weak points. The weak point in the German mind, seen from an historical standpoint, is its amorphous expansionism and its mediaeval anachronism, to which only the idea of German national unity in a limited nation-state is opposed.

Political warfare is politics. It is not propaganda made in a vacuum without any clear idea of the political objective to be achieved. War, as Clausewitz correctly observed — and many others observed before him — is merely politics in another sphere; it is the *ultima ratio* of politics. We have this war to fight because in a generation we have never had any politics — either vis-à-vis Europe or vis-à-vis the Far East. We have merely had *modus vivendi*.

We have done the wrong things — from Versailles, Saint-Germain, and Trianon to Munich — because we could not see what right things to do.

Seeing the right things to do is to conduct political warfare of such a nature that victory will mean a political clarification and not another muddle. There are sins of omission as well as sins of commission. On that count, we all stand accused before history. If the German mind is muddled, as it certainly is, and this war is an attempt to break through a muddle by the most utter violence, it is well that we place reason, realism, and clarity behind our arms, lest out of the conflict of various muddles we blow up the whole earth in a futility of destruction.

III

GEOGRAPHY AND THE GERMAN MIND

HAVING MADE, in this condensed way, telescoping into a few pages what needs volumes — but the volumes would never be read by wide numbers of people — some facts and conclusions about German history and its effect on the German mind, let us survey the German mind from another vantage-point, namely, that of geography.

For the German mind, like German history, is partly the creation of geographical factors.

And let us bear in mind that our object here, is not to make anti-German propaganda for the consumption of Americans and Englishmen, but to study with the most objective realism the factors contributing to the mind which we wish to understand and influence.

Germany, as we have seen in a survey of her history, is a nation that has never yet established and consolidated her frontiers to her own satisfaction.

THE ANALOGY WITH SPARTA

In more ways than one she thus resembles ancient Sparta, and it is probably no coincidence that in her present phase, when she is trying to be all her conflicting selves at one time, she should have copied the Spartan pattern almost to the last detail.

The other Hellenic states found *Lebensraum*, as other European states have since done, by discovery, conquest, and colonization overseas, a process which got them into no trouble with their neighbors and involved no excessive military effort.

But the Spartans, when they felt the need for more room, did not turn their eyes to the sea like the Chalcidians, or Corinthians, or Megarians. The sea was not visible from Sparta City or from any point on the Spartan plain, or even from the heights that surround it. Sparta was landlocked, not sea-locked, as Germany, unlike France, Spain, Italy, Scandinavia, to say nothing of Britain, but like Russia, is pre-eminently a country of land frontiers, its seacoast its shortest border, and that upon the North Sea and the Baltic, and not upon the open ocean.

Sparta, like Germany, therefore, set out to conquer her neighbors rather than seek outlets across the seas. To prepare herself for this purpose, she created a military and racial state which conquered the entire Hellenic world.

But having conquered it, Sparta was utterly unable to organize and rule it satisfactorily. The very system which had made her invincible in war made her sterile in peace. She became frozen in her own militarism and rigidities, and the Spartan epoch is an epoch without a history. Centuries after Rome, in her turn, had conquered the Hellenic world, the question of the very frontier over which the original Spartan war started — her Polish Corridor — was settled before a Roman tribunal — and against the Spartans.[1]

Military expansionism is an historic characteristic of more than one land power. In the case of modern Germany, it has been the rampant characteristic of the army-founded German state as it was the persistent characteristic of the Austro-Hungarian and Ottoman Empires. It will be a menace as long as the German nation is geographically expansionist. The German concept of continental power to be won at the expense of her neighbors is similar to the concept of Sparta and to the concept of Napoleon. The Czechs are Germany's Africans, the Poles her helots.

Germany has maintained a situation where the state is conceived of as an army — whether that state is capitalist or socialist. 'Prussian Socialism,' so-called by Oswald Spengler, is nothing except the socialism of an army, which is, indeed, an organization freed of any taint of the personal-profit motive.

THE GEO-POLITICAL POSITION OF GERMANY

In the case of Germany, militarism is more than a menace to Europe and Russia. It is a menace to the whole world, increased by the geographic position of Germany.

After the last war one of the most eminent of British

---

[1] For the most brilliant short study of Sparta, see Arnold F. Toynbee's *A Study of History*, vol. III. Oxford University Press.

geographers, Sir Halford Mackinder, then professor at Oxford, wrote a little book called *Democratic Ideals and Reality*.[1] This book, republished in the last months, attracted so much attention in England at the time of its original publication that the author sold the whole of eight hundred copies! Where it did attract attention was in Germany, where geo-politics have always been understood by a militarist society.   Sir Halford, trying to warn his own blind countrymen, only succeeded in giving a few tips to General Haushofer, the German geo-politician. Sir Halford had the same experience as Charles de Gaulle.

The major thesis of Mackinder's little book is that there are not five 'continents' in any strictly geographical sense, but one, the Great Continent, which embraces Eurasia and Africa, and contains the overwhelming majority of the population and resources of the planet; that this continent, off which even the Americas appear as mere islands, can be conquered from a central land position or 'heartland'; that this 'heartland' lies in Russia and around the Black Sea,[2] through the Middle East, and is the gate to both Asia and Africa; that who holds this 'heartland' is in a world central position; and that it is absolutely necessary, therefore, to build a strong federation of non-German and non-Russian states between Germany and Russia, since the juncture of the two countries, either by the

[1] Sir Halford Mackinder, *Democratic Ideals and Reality*.   Henry Holt and Company, New York.

[2] Napoleon also said, 'Constantinople is the key to the world.'

conquest of one over the other, or by aggressive alliance between them, would constitute a world-wide menace, occupying the crucial geographical position, and extremely difficult to defeat by non-military nations depending upon sea power.

Sir Halford's warning was utterly ignored at the peace table and in the subsequent post-war years. Instead of a strong federation of eastern non-German and non-Russian states, the new nations of the East were an unorganized complex of fundamentally weak states, and an open invitation was thus given the Germans again to try their hands at world conquest.

For a military-minded nation to be thus confronted and tempted by opportunity was another of the political mistakes for which the whole earth suffers today.

COLONIAL VERSUS CONTIGUOUS EXPANSION

It cannot be too strongly stressed that Hitler was inventing nothing new when he demanded at the outset of his movement 'contiguous land territory capable of supporting millions of Germans' — colonies in the heart of Europe and Eurasia itself. Nor is that concept unique to the Nazis, Napoleon, or Europe. It was cherished by the northern United States both before and after the Civil War — the idea of the South as an internal colony and granary for the rest of the nation. It was one cause of the Civil War, and only in our generation has the concept begun to be rectified, by the triumph of the real anti-slavery idea implicit in 'one nation indivisible with liberty and justice for all.'

Hitler has made it clear that he does not believe in overseas colonies, however much he may have demanded them or advanced the lack of them as an excuse for other *Lebensraum* plans.[1]

Also the era of colonial expansionism for the rest of Europe coincided with the time that Germany was a Bund of separated dynastically governed states. There were certain colonial enterprises in this period, like that of the 'Great Kurfurst,' who attempted to found a colony in Africa in the seventeenth century. But this, like others, was the enterprise of a king of a petty state, not a national enterprise. When Germany was welded into a national state in 1870, the possibilities of great extensions in overseas territories were pretty well exhausted.

This sense of coming late into history is part of the German mind, giving it at once a feeling of inferiority and frustration with a counter-compensation of being young, and therefore a ban-breaker. *Die Sendung der Jungen Völker* (*The Mission of the Young Peoples*) [2] is not only the title of an influential modern German book, but an expression of belief in the mission of a young nation to destroy traditional forms and create new ones.

Yet, the conception of the conquest of the East is as we have seen not new, and in no sense is it revolutionary.

[1] See *Mein Kampf*.   [2] Ernst Jünger.

The German *colonization* of the Slavic East — in the Baltic, in Poland, in southeastern Europe, and even so far into Russia as the Volga — was not originally a national enterprise of either Prussia or Austria. Again it preceded the birth of the German nation by centuries. In the Baltic countries it was an enterprise of the Order of Teutonic Knights, who used Christianity as a sword against the 'barbarians' *and conquered for themselves and not for Germany.* The Fuehrer Schools of the S.S. are a modern attempt to revive the spirit of these ideological conquerors of the East. These boys of middle-class parents are being consciously educated as a new aristocracy and 'knighthood' for conquest and administration.

In the Balkans there was no organized colonization, but rather a migration of southern German tribes of Saxons and Swabians who went to Hungary and parts of the South Slav world (Jugoslavia) and Rumania, establishing settlements there without reference to any political power. Afterward, these settlements were used by political powers for imperialist, contiguous-empire purposes; by Austria in the Balkans, by Prussia in the Baltic, and pre-eminently by Hitler, whose claim to eastern Europe is based in part upon these scattered settlements. He has, of course, used them everywhere for fifth-column activities.

Geographically, Germany is set in a predominantly Slavic world that for centuries she has been trying to push back; but never successfully, for though waves went east, counter-waves came west, and the German population is full of Slavic blood, and German culture full of Slavic characteristics.

A cleavage in the German mind comes from the fact that in all the centuries German intentions toward the East could not be *absolutely* clarified. And never was the German assault upon the Slavic world permanently successful. Bismarck attempted to Germanize the Polish provinces of Poznan and Pomerellen. They belonged to the German Reich as an integral part of it for well over a century, and they were systematically colonized by Germany. Yet, in 1918 they were still overwhelmingly Polish, both in population, language, and national feelings.

The Austro-Hungarian Empire, with its concept of domination over the 'inferior races' of the Southeast, broke up during the last war, as we have seen, by internal disintegration and collapse caused by the risings of the subject peoples.

The popular fact contributing to the failure of both the Prussians and Austrians was that the German people *did not like the East*. Their real longing was for the West. Neither Austrian Germans, Prussian Germans, nor any other Germans longed to settle down in a predominantly Slavic world.

The Germanic population in the East steadily decreased; under the German Republic there was an 'eastern problem,' and land corps and heavily subsidized settlement schemes had to be organized under patriotic impetus to persuade youthful Germans to settle in the eastern provinces and take over the work of Polish and other 'foreign' agricultural laborers. Even the existing *Lebensraum* in the East was shunned. The push toward the East was a Prussian Junker-landowner-military idea and the idea of an expansionist aristocratically ruled Austria.

There is another geographical, or rather demographical, fact that stood, and stands, in the way of Germany's policy of creating an empire at the expense of her neighbors.

The *Lebensraum* in the East that she is conquering is not, as North America, or Australia, or South Africa were, sparsely populated by savage tribes. It is among the most thickly populated areas of Europe. It is inhabited by European peasants, with old traditions. To afford room for a vast overflow of Germanic population — for which Hitler claims necessity — not only must land be conquered, but populations must be moved or exterminated. In eastern Europe, southeastern Europe, and European Russia are approximately one hundred and forty million non-Germanic peoples, predominantly Slavic and peasant or land-dwelling, and with a natural birth-rate much higher than that of the Germans.

These peoples have lived historically under many empires, but they went through an immense national awakening in 1918, and belong themselves to the 'Young Peoples.' The resistance of Serbian Jugoslavia in this war is the fiercest to be offered by any small nation, as the Russian resistance is the fiercest of any large nation and the fight of the Polish legions the most passionate of any completely defeated nation, while the Czechs continue stubbornly resistant.

The resistance of the eastern peoples is the resistance of nations who know what it means to be conquered. They have an historical experience behind them. Serbia remembers Kossovo and the Turks.[1]

These nations know that conquest by the Germans means extermination and slavery in the exact meaning of those words. *Otherwise the conquest makes no sense to the Germans.*

WHAT EASTERN CONQUEST MEANS TO THE GERMAN PEOPLE

But what *does* it mean to the German people? To the German masses?

To the party leaders it means administrative posts; to German industrialists it means industrial control over vast areas and monopolized markets. But to the German people, it means a never-ending struggle, in which they must lead the life of Caesar's legions, far from home, never demobilized, a frontier life, requiring immense and continuing force. Eastern Europe cannot be governed, as Britain's empire in its heyday was, by a division or two, money, and

[1] See Rebecca West's *Black Lamb and Grey Falcon* (Viking Press), probably the greatest book to be written since this war began.

the prestige of white men over 'natives.' It would have to be held as Sparta tried to hold her empire, and the cost would be the price Sparta paid: she was bled white by it.

Victory, in Hitler's war, could not be satisfactorily consolidated for generations, if ever. It is a fallacy to have literates and Europeans as helots. It would have to be sustained for generations by force. The Reich of a Thousand Years means that sort of Reich.

And what would be the effect on German culture? What is the effect of any imperialism on a national culture?

Even an overseas empire, consolidated among peoples who have no national history or culture to oppose to their invaders and actually have their standard of living lifted by the conquerors, drains the best blood and brains of a nation. Such empire once meant hunting parks and bank accounts for a relatively small number of Britishers, but, in the long run, poverty and disemployment for more.

In all the 'old' empires there is a strong conviction that empire nowadays does not pay.

But such a 'contiguous empire' as Hitler's *Ost-Politik* envisages, among peoples with strong national aspirations and superior in numbers and birth-rate to the German, would result in a tremendous admixture of blood, a terrible waste of young manhood used up in its suppression and administration, and an unremitting sword-and-fire policy, *with the inevitable corruption of German culture and the German mind and soul.*

There are plenty of Germans who know this, and are as apprehensive of victory as they are of defeat. Even thoughtful officers in the German Army seriously doubt whether it is possible to keep any European and nationally conscious people permanently conquered, and they know what the cost of keeping them permanently conquered is.

WHAT PRICE GLORY?

German workers are already seeing their factories filled with Slavic and other foreign workers — six million of them by August, 1942 — while their brothers and sons perform the 'heroic' task of losing their lives or serving as armies of occupation in miserable outposts far from home. What price glory?

The Nazi authorities are already gravely concerned with the problem of their own paucity of population in view of such an empire. They are abandoning the Pure Germanic Race theory, and actually experimenting with forced interbreeding between picked German youth and picked physical examples of the races they have conquered. But what price to the German girl at home, who sees the man she hoped to marry mated off with a stronger and more beautiful Polish or French girl? What price to the youth, who, having fought in a dozen campaigns, sits in Omsk or Pinsk or Belgrade or Korosten, yearning for Stuttgart or Lindau — for Mosel wine and Eisbein, for linden trees and the neat farmyard, for the devoted Mutti, and the family around the piano? What price to the wife, learning that her husband, in Norway or France, is now permitted to take an 'honorary wife' to bear him extra children, in order to increase the breed of conquerors and administrators?

'Hans,' I am sure, sees all this. Conquest brings corruption and despair. *There is no sense in it all.*

This apprehension brings another cleavage in the German mind. It fears defeat, but it also unconsciously fears victory. The fear of defeat is not so strong in the German mind at present, but the unconscious fear of victory *is* there.

Germany sees her territory widening and her culture, her home life, her happiness going to pieces. The contiguous empire yawns like an abyss, beckoning one moment, threatening the next. And it has not been made sufficiently clear what a Hitler victory would mean to Germany.

That is our business: the business of political warfare. To conduct such political warfare convincingly, one must, of course, be intellectually convinced oneself that a victory for Hitler would be the end of Germany — as well as the end of all of us.

ANOTHER LEBENSRAUM

But one must be prepared to keep alive in the German mind the vision of another *Lebensraum*, in a place where she is not looking for it at present.

That *Lebensraum* exists. It exists for Germany in exactly the same sphere where other advanced nations can find it in the twentieth-century world — neither in contiguous empire nor in empire overseas; nor in areas to be exploited by monopolistic enterprise, capitalist or state capitalist; nor in places where the best blood of peoples must be wasted in armies of occupation; nor in the subjection of human work-slaves or nations of peoples who constantly threaten to revolt, and who, if only passively resistant, continually sabotage.

The whole concept of *Lebensraum* by conquest of other peoples, whether Kiplingesque or Hitlerite, is preposterous because it is now archaic. It had a realistic and materialistic justification once, however offensive it may have been to man's higher moral nature. It has no justification whatsoever today.

Plato's observation that all high civilizations had been, and must in the nature of things continue to be, founded upon slavery — a great source which the Nazis constantly quote to justify themselves — was a bleak but true observation as of his day. It is still a true observation, but with a difference. Man in our century has created his slaves, not of flesh and blood, but of steel, rubber, and synthetic materials equal to them. Mankind is in possession of millions and millions of serfs, who ask nothing but subsistence, who respond to orders with invariable docility, who have neither minds to question nor hearts to revolt: perfect slaves. They are machines.

Since the intellectual and moral development of the human race as a whole is somewhere back in the dark ages, while the development of man's science through the work of relatively few brains is in the present century, we continue to live in a political order, and to follow ideas, which are not dead only because the ignorance of mankind and the vested interests of politicians and others, continue to keep them artificially alive.

Human slavery of any kind must be abolished because mechanical slavery has come. The mechanical slaves are better than the human slaves. Mankind can at long last be — if they want to be — civilized and humane at the same time. This is the remarkable fact of our century.

Furthermore, the *Lebensraum* of raw materials is being expanded every day in the laboratories of chemists and physicists, where, in the words of Doctor Charles Stine, vice-president of the DuPont de Nemours Company, and himself a distinguished chemist, 'we are discovering *new continents* of matter.' And these new continents are not only being discovered in American laboratories; they are daily being discovered in German laboratories. Atomic physics and transmutation of elements in the field of chemistry are creating new matter and inexhaustible energies. The Nazi war is, therefore, not merely a wicked war; it is an idiotic war — which makes it even more wicked, since reason must, I think, be counted among man's moral attributes.

This fact has certainly not passed unobserved by the German mind. It produces a cleavage in it, a cleavage which we must systematically widen. For the German mind, despite its historical *mystique* and its geographical influences, is also a scientific mind. And the scientific spirit should be made into our ally.

IV

GERMAN RATIONALISM AND THE
SCIENTIFIC SPIRIT

BUT before we can make it into our ally, let us ana-
lyze — again as objectively as we can and without a trace of
rancor — what there is in the structure of the present world,
and especially of Europe, which militates against our allying
that mind on our side as long as we fail to clarify certain
principles; what questions must be answered if we are to
mobilize that mind in the political sphere.

The scientific attitude is questioning and analytical.

The facts of German experience, viewed by such a mind,
make it radical. And science has contributed to its skepticism and radicalism.

The German scientific mind is skeptical of all existing
political systems, and German experience has confirmed its
doubts.

Within the lifetime of every adult German, he has seen
three political systems fail. The Empire of the Hohenzol-
lerns seemed founded upon a rock. It fell. The Weimar
Republic was born in defeat, yet it managed to make Germany again the leading industrial power of Europe and
more united than ever before in her history, and it com-

manded during at least half of its lifetime the allegiance of ninety per cent of the German people. It fell.

The Nazi Reich is nearly ten years old. In the seventh year it plunged Germany into another world war. Will it last?

The fact that Hitler feels that he has to assure the German people over and over again that it will is indicative. Also indicative is the fact that lately Hitler has reduced his prophecy. The 'thousand years' has become two hundred!

A skeptical German like Hjalmar Schacht once made a witty and almost untranslatable remark, '*Die tausend Jahre des dritten Reiches verrinnen mit jüdischer Hast.*' [1] (The 'thousand years' of the Third Reich trickle away with Jewish busyness.)

The German mind in the last generation has been subjected to a whole series of tremendous shocks: the loss of the first war; the inflation, which wiped out the entire financial structure of the Reich; the depression, which plunged a renascent country into a despair as great as the loss of the war; the new war, which Hitler promised would not come. Characteristic, therefore, of this mind is that it doubts everything. The German historical past is doubtful; the present is awful; the future is something that cannot be contemplated, *no matter how the war turns out.*

This lack of a sense of stability is certainly partly respon-

---

[1] 'Jüdische Hast' means the urgency that some Gentiles associate with Jewish nervousness — active, febrile, fussy.

sible for the willingness to accept despotic authority as a refuge. 'The love of the jellyfish for the rock.'

But the German scientific and rational spirit, which might be our ally, is also extremely dangerous to us. It leads men to perform the tasks at hand amazingly well, regardless of the purposes to which they are put. There is still another cleavage in the German mind: its ability to divorce the task from the purpose.

In the days of the Republic, German communists openly advocated the destruction of the entire capitalist system. But that did not prevent them from working admirably in the factories.

I have a friend in Germany who bitterly hates this war and ardently hopes that Nazi Germany will lose it. (This is not 'Hans.') But that does not prevent him from doing the most precise scientific work in the perfection of airplane equipment with which to bomb the peoples of nations that he adores.

The German, who has never been wholly satisfied with any political system under which he has lived or which he historically knows about, is a perfectionist as a worker, lives in his work, and manages to divide himself into two parts: the part that renders unto Caesar, and the part that does homage to work, science, and art, and retains 'inner freedom.' The Russian says, 'You have my body, but not my soul.' So does the German.

The German is a thinking being. No people in Europe

are more so. (He makes war scientifically, unfortunately
for us. Unlike West Point, German military schools have a
rigorous training in geo-politics. German officers really
know that the earth is round: something very unfortunate
for us, who have not yet fully grasped that fact, even in the
army, to say nothing of the United States Congress. Like
the Russians he knows that it is round both ways — around
the north and the south, as well as around the east and the
west.)

The German has an immense respect for just one thing
and confidence in just one thing: precise work. Whether in
the field of science, war, agriculture, technology, or manual
labor, his thoroughness is a by-word.

He knows that he is second to few on earth as a worker,
and he has a very revelatory word: *Arbeitsfreude* — joy in
work.

It is this that makes the Germans, like the Japanese,
formidable enemies. It is this that makes them eminent
geographers, superb producers, great organizers. They are
meticulous about details; they plan carefully, never proceed-
ing by rule of thumb. I am sure that someone in Germany
knows where every oil well on earth is located and what its
average production has been over the last twenty years.
They are the world's greatest cartographers, and I cherish
old German maps because I cannot get anything like as
good ones now.

They are great workers under whatever form of government they have. Hitler may speak of the *Truemmerhaufen* (scrap heap) of the Republic, but the *Truemmerhaufen* existed in the German mind, not in reality. Actually what the German Republic accomplished was a miracle.

But it is this, their genuine gift, which to a thoughtful German must make their conquests the more silly.

Their scientific gifts and their industry have made them great — not their political confusion, messianism, and militarism. Their industriousness has made them Europe's greatest industrial people. This has come out of themselves, not out of conquest and loot, and they have every reason to be proud of it.

If it gives them a superiority complex, as it certainly and irritatingly does, it must also raise questions in the rational German mind.

For in any straight competition with other peoples, not backed up by arms, mobilizing the world against them, they know they have a good chance to meet all comers.

The German scientist, or technologist, or industrialist knows that it is a great deal cheaper to buy raw materials, of which there is a plethora on this earth, than to send good workers out to conquer them. Also he knows that 'blood and soil' are not the sources of twentieth-century power. We live in a world where we can turn milk into wool and plastic, air into fertilizer, acetyline gas into wood, trees into stockings, and, unfortunately, nearly anything into explosives.

While German boys are dying like flies for soil, German scientists are conquering new continents out of the matter all around them.

Poverty of resources has not made the German poor. It has made him *resourceful*.

The greatest things accomplished by Germany have all been done by the overcoming of natural obstacles, and their gifts to the world have been immense. Every day of our lives we profit in some way by German inventions; we shall even have to defeat them with many of their own formulas.

This rational and scientific mind has made the Germans impatient of the present organization of the earth, which they consider anarchic and archaic. They believe that they have a mission in its reconstruction.

They also want to be loved and admired for their qualities. Politically and historically uncertain, they are certain of their creative abilities through work in all its phases.

Today they are using those abilities in a manner that has made them hated of mankind, and this fact must produce psychological sufferings, however overcompensated they may be.

One compensation that serves them is the suspicion that the world hates them because of their positive and creative qualities as well as their negative ones; that the world is trying to destroy serious competitors; that rather than rise to their standard of exact work and energetic labor, the world would like to remove them.

Unfortunately, this apprehension is supported by suggestions emanating from persons in this country and elsewhere that Germany, after the war, and in order to prevent her rearmament and another aggression, be de-industrialized.

Now, if it be truly so that all indications brand the Germans as incorrigible and that no political system can be invented which will render them harmless to other peoples, then the suggestion is realistic, though nobody has yet suggested just how it is to be permanently enforced. But this much is certain: If a people are forbidden to exercise those talents and gifts which they possess to a superior degree and which could enrich the world and not impoverish it, they are driven to a resistance fanatical to the point where they will destroy themselves and everyone else rather than yield.

The idea of de-industrialization is backed by some representatives of small nations who are aware of the superiority of Germany in this field.

But given any rationalism in a coming political order, based upon our victory, such a program would strike at us all, for every talent and every skill is an asset to the whole planet if it is used *for* the world instead of *against* it.

And it is the clear picture of such a mutual use of skills and talents for the new *Lebensraum* of the twentieth century which must be held out to the rational mind of the Germans, if we wish to secure their collaboration in abandoning the present program of conquest. If we are not looking for their collaboration, then the political warfare of reasonable persuasion is aimless. And the political warfare of threat will militate against us. For if the Germans think they face annihilation, either as a nation or as a working society, all our propaganda, as to our own strength and the certainty of their defeat, far from discouraging them, will encourage them to gird up their loins for a struggle to the death.

And if we are going to appeal to German rationalism, then we must admit the necessity for a radical reorganization of Europe in the future, and abandon once and for all the idea of re-establishing anything approaching the former *status quo.*

For not only the German mind, but the rational European mind, has been in revolt for a generation against certain factors in the political and economic organization of Europe.

Among the Four Freedoms, one is not mentioned. It is one of the essential personal freedoms of mankind: freedom to move. For a generation, ever since the last war, neither persons nor goods could move in Europe with any fluidity whatsoever. A customs frontier confronted the European in every few hours of travel. The necessity for a labor permit made it all but impossible for him to sell his labor or his services anywhere outside the frontiers of his own nation. More than a score of armies and hordes of officials ate up the substance of European taxpayers. Economic and military autonomy were synonymous with political autonomy all over Europe.

The rational German mind and the rational European mind have been in revolt against that state of affairs since long before Hitler. This does not mean that the mere establishment of Europe as a free-trade area would solve all its economic problems. The establishment of the United States as a free-trade area has not solved our problems, and it has even increased the economic problems of parts of the nation, for instance, the South.

But a rationalization of the European economy is necessary both for the more primitive nations and for highly developed ones. Free trade would be successful and promote economic justice only if combined with a more reasonable distribution of industry and a greater rationalization of both industry and agriculture. The scientific mind revolts at the realization that in Rumania, for instance, thousands of acres of highly fertile land are worked in the twentieth century with the tools and habits of the sixteenth.

And not only to scientifically minded Germans, but also to rational Europeans as a whole, the necessity for greater European unity has been obvious for many generations. It was not Hitler, but Nietzsche, who despised the Germans, who cried, 'Europe must unite or perish.' It was not Mussolini, with his dream of a restoration of the power of Rome, who cried for European federation, but a much greater Italian, Mazzini, who fought in vain for a united Italy in a federated Europe. And in our own times, the great French liberal and humanist, Romaine Rolland, has cried, 'Europe must broaden or perish.'

German rationalism revolts against balance-of-power politics pursued in so small a framework as the nations of Europe — and not *German* rationalism alone. In our day, and on our own side, European statesmen and intellectuals are calling for a United Nations policy which supports European unity in a single federation, or, as a first step, in a series of interlocking and overlapping federations of the Scandinavian, southern European, Germanic, eastern European, Balkan, and western nations.

I left Paris, as it was falling, with the words of one of Mussolini's greatest opponents ringing in my ears — the words of a man who, when the day of freedom comes, will surely play a rôle in Italy. 'Unless the Allies act, Hitler will one day proclaim the United States of Europe. It will be a swindle, but it will nevertheless attract many Europeans.'

Rational Europeans consider that Europe has two enemies: those who want to keep her broken up and divided, and those who want to dominate her.

And this confuses the issues of the war, both in the German mind and in the European mind as a whole.

Progressive teachers in Germany for generations before Hitler — those teachers who were least 'Prussian' and least nationalist and chauvinist — taught students that Napoleon had a great idea in striving for the unification of the continent, *even at the expense of Germany*. The attitude was: Well, it might have been a good thing if he had won. His methods were rotten, his spirit was egotistic and destructive, the idea of French hegemony was absurd, but had he succeeded he would at least have wiped out dynastic ambitions, and afterward a more reasonable Europe with liberty and justice for all could have been created.

Thus, to many German opponents of the Third Reich today, Hitler appears in the paradoxical rôle of the Angel of Destruction, the Judas who nevertheless may serve the interests of the Master, like Attila a 'scourge of God' whose historic rôle it will be to call Europe and the world to its senses, in opposing and defeating him.

And many Germans think of Hitler as Faust's Mephisto, whom Goethe described as 'Ein Teil von jener Kraft die stets das Böse will, und doch das Gute schafft.' (A part of that Force that wills evil and yet creates the good.)

We are in serious danger today of confronting Europe, not with a solution which seems rational to her, but with a choice of two evils, whether to be unified by force and exploited by a master nation — the more intolerable — or reduced again to the anarchy of more than a score of independent and sovereign states still divided by customs frontiers, each supporting petty armies, and recognizing no common law above themselves.

Even the Germans who know that Hitler's program is terrible and ruinous nevertheless ask: What program *does* make sense?

Many Europeans including non-Nazi Germans have expected, no, have hoped and prayed, that a proposal for a large solution would come from the United States of America. Why, they have argued, should the United States, which is a great continental nation, be interested in re-creating in Europe everything abolished by the American Constitution in North America, more than one hundred and fifty years ago?

Yet, the American mind is narrow and pessimistic regarding Europe. The Atlantic Charter does not close the door to European federation, but it certainly does not open it. And to a European, whether German or otherwise, it does not go beyond Woodrow Wilson's rights of self-determination that, as worked out in 1918–33, spelled anarchy. The Atlantic Charter offers national solutions, but no European solution. Europe has moved a long way since Woodrow Wilson and gone through the bitterest experiences, culminating in the total incapacity of the small nations, after eating up their substance with armies for a quarter of a century, to defend themselves.

The lack of any systematic policy on the European or world question — any clear war aims — leaves a vacuum into which publicists like Professor Renner can move, with his *Maps for a New World*, in which small nations are completely shattered and swallowed by the European great powers — a pure Italian-Fascist solution; or into which statesmen like Herbert Hoover and Hugh Gibson can move, with their book on *Problems of Lasting Peace*, which is basically timid and pessimistic and actually seems partially to accept Hitler's racist theory of tribal organization of Europe, advocating that we have the 'audacity' to transfer whole populations from one area to another, thereby putting ourselves — or rather themselves — on the side of one of the most unpopular acts that Hitler is committing.

The suggestion swimming about in the ether, that after the war there will be some sort of Anglo-American police system for Europe, is almost as infuriating to other Europeans as to Germans. The European nations must be liberated and helped to reorganize themselves as Europeans into a modern federative system, which eliminates balance-of-power politics on continental Europe and ends the anarchy that has prevailed since 1914. Basic to this are, of course, the twin ideas basic to the whole of western civilization and nowhere more revered or incorporated into the life of a nation than in America: Freedom and Equality.

European federalism, in one form or another, would also help to solve the German national and political problem. The fact that, like the United States, the German nation is really a combination of many states, and, indeed, many Germanies, and that its culture has always flourished best in a decentralized system — as, indeed, most cultures do — inclines a great many Germans toward a Germanic federation, implicit in an all-European system whose unity would, among other things, permit of much greater diversity.

Highly centralized large states are created for purposes of monopoly and militarism.

In such a Germanic federation, the widely differing cultures of Austria and Catholic Germany, the Hanseatic merchant communities, and the northern and eastern provinces could have fuller play. Essential to a genuine federal system for Germany would be the reduction of the state of Prussia. This state has steadily enlarged itself, by the absorption of neighboring states, until it dominates the Reich. In the pre-war Reich of sixty-five million it encompassed three-fifths of the population, and the danger of such a compact power was recognized by the Weimar Constitution. In the Republic's parliament, Prussia could control a majority, and in the upper house, or Reichsrat, where votes were otherwise apportioned according to population, Prussia was only allowed two-fifths of the votes.

In the present Reich — excluding the non-Germans, of course, who have been acquired as 'contiguous colonies' — Prussia still encompasses fifty per cent of the population, and as a compact power could control a majority.

Rational Europeans, including Germans, are federalists. Such Europeans are the carriers of the real revolutionary spirit of tomorrow — the revolution of reason, realism, and humanism.

They are open to the concept of being 'Americanized,' in so far as America represents in their minds the concept of federalism and equality in union under law. But they do not want to look forward to being 'policed' by the Anglo-American world.

And no simple duplication of the American pattern is possible or advisable. Europe is composed of nations, of national states; they are the substance of Europe and the source of her creative diversity and cultural depth. A monolithic Europe, wiping out deep-rooted and diverse characteristics of culture and mind-forms, would represent brittle and superficial power and be a great loss to western civilization. Revolutions which drastically destroy historical continuity and cultural accumulations are disasters.

If we appeal to the scientific and rational spirit, we must appeal with scientific reason and rational objectivity. And we must be bold enough to risk offending politicians, some of whom have a vested interest in restoration movements of one kind or another. Only thus can we come into contact with the scientific and rational spirit of Germany.

V

THE REVELATIONS OF GERMAN CULTURE

IN OUR RECONNAISSANCE of the German mind, let us make at least a superficial survey of German culture: of its philosophy, literature, and art.

Here, as in its history, we find evidence of the divided German personality.

With all apologies to Lord Vansittart — a man whom I greatly admire, and who is one of the Englishmen who realizes most clearly that German 'daemonism' cannot be attributed to the Treaty of Versailles, but can be traced back for at least a century, and who knows, furthermore, that ideas move the universe at least as much as economics do — the book which he edited of quotations from the world of German 'poets and thinkers,' showing Germany as perennially hellbent on conquest and destruction, could be offset, quotation for quotation, by other writers of equal influence, showing just the opposite.

ITS PARADOXES

The tensions in the German mind, the polarities induced by her social inheritance, have made it, as we have tried to demonstrate, a paradoxical mind. Some of her most influential writers display the same paradoxes in themselves and especially in their interpreters. The philosopher, Hegel, for instance, is regarded as an ideological founder of the Prussian military state, a conception which the American military writer, Homer Lea, could praise as 'truly sublime.' Sublime or not, Hegel has been used to justify the Prussian concept of a state based on discipline and obedience and inclusive of the whole of life. The Nazis can, with some shred of truth, claim to be walking in his path — they can claim to be walking in almost any path. But Hegel was certainly the logician of Karl Marx, whom the Nazis regard as their bitterest philosophic enemy. And Karl Marx, also, was a German and though not an 'Aryan' he was much more German than Jewish. He was not anti-Semitic, but he actually was anti-Judaistic.

Another profoundly influential German spirit, Nietzsche, was never able to reconcile the contradictions in his own mind, and died mad. His virulent hatred of Germany may have been unconsciously a hatred of his own mental tortures.

It is right in Prussia, too, that one finds the greatest paradoxes. If Prussia produced Hegel, the parent of the Prussian state and the creator of Marxian logics, it is in Prussia, and even in East Prussia, that one finds that world mind and humanistic spirit, Kant, with his concept of the moral order as the only ultimate imperative.

If it is true that Field Marshal General Ewald von Kleist,

a Prussian Junker from a long line of Prussian Junker officers, fell in the Caucasus fighting Hitler's war for *Lebensraum*, a funeral oration might be said over his grave in behalf of the United Nations, and the words of that oration be written by his greatest ancestor, the German poet, Bernd Heinrich Wilhelm von Kleist, who, like his family before and after him, served in the Prussian Army.

Yet Kleist, writing during the Napoleonic Wars, when Prussia was an ally of Britain and one of the United Nations resisting domination, pleaded for war aims that today, in the mouth of a Henry Wallace, would be called Utopian. He felt that the unity of Europe, established in the face of a common foe seeking to impose his own personal and national hegemony, should be the precursor to a new world unity based on freedom and equality. He wrote — and thousands of Germans have read his words in their school readers:

> Is our stake the same as that in other wars which have been fought over the face of the earth? Is it for the glory of some ambitious prince that we fight? Is ours a campaign alike to those of the War of the Spanish Succession, directed like moves on a chessboard, where hearts do not throb, emotions are not whipped by passions, and where the poison arrows of insult do not cause muscles to twitch? Do we fight for the cession of a province, the dispute of some claim? Or to exact payment of a debt, or some other object ... possessed today, given up tomorrow, reacquired the day after tomorrow?
>
> No! Our stake is a commonwealth, whose roots ... strike deep in the soil of time. ... A commonwealth which, foreign to the spirit of lust for power or conquest, is worthy of existing

and worthy of the submission to be rendered it. *A common-wealth which cannot conceive of any glory for itself unless that glory embraces all others and the welfare of all who dwell upon this earth. ... A commonwealth set up by the free choice of brother nations. A commonwealth, in a word, which belongs to the whole human race, and which even the wild natives of the South Seas would rally to defend.*

I do not say that Kleist was a typical Prussian Junker, but he was a by no means untypical German. He was representative of the world idea of freedom and equality, for nations and for men, kindled first on this soil by the American Revolution and a few years later in Europe by the French, gone sour then in militant nationalism, and represented in Germany by such works as Schiller's *Don Carlos*, and *An die Freude*. This spirit was, to Europe's unutterable misfortune, betrayed and crushed by Metternich, Castlereagh, and Alexander, as the spirit of the United Nations, not yet kindled to the magnitude of the crisis and opportunity, may again be crushed by men of little faith, in the peace.

The formula of Hegel, thesis — antithesis — synthesis, which confirms that action produces reaction and both are harmonized eventually, reveals the German consciousness of paradox and the hope, out of paradox, to achieve harmony.

Harmony it seldom finds, however. The German mind tends to exaggeration: to be all out in one direction or the other; it lacks measure. German philosophical systems are intuitive and deductive rather than inductive — *vide* Leibnitz, Hegel, Kant, Goethe, Schopenhauer, Spengler. They are idealistic. They are not empirical, utilitarian, or pragmatic, like the English and American, and not precise and logical like the French. They strive, also, to embrace the universe, and to find universal solutions for things.

German philosophy is in sharpest contrast to the petty small middle-class spirit which characterized much of German social and political life before and after the last war, and which supported Hitler. It is also far from the 'folkish' spirit, out of which grows perhaps the only popular culture of Germany — the culture of her folklore. The great German philosophies are not 'German,' except in spirit. They are in no sense national. They are less to be defined nationally than most philosophies, such as the British, which keeps a fairly consistent empirical line. The philosophy of England is practical. The philosophy of France is logical. The philosophy of Germany is imaginative. Hegel's state is no more the Prussian state than Plato's state was the Greek state. It is a sublime and idealistic conception, heartily disagreeable to a Jeffersonian, who sees in the state one of the eternal enemies of human freedom. Yet it was also a modern German, Franz Oppenheim, who wrote a book on *The State* which is Jeffersonism acceptable to a man like Albert Nock, who is more Jeffersonian than Jefferson.

Are we to believe that a mind so universal and so world-embracing, and so paradoxical as well, speaking out of a people with a history so episodic and contradictory, has reached its final apotheosis in Naziism? In Hitler's 'Thousand-Year Reich'? Or in the military Prussian state? To believe so is to accept the Nazi thesis — that Naziism is the 'true' and final face of Germany. It is quite impossible for me to believe it. The greatest German minds have conceived of Germany and the human race as 'Becoming'; the protean consciousness of growth and change is profoundly characteristic of most of them. Especially, for instance, of Goethe.

A UNIVERSAL CULTURE WITHOUT A GERMAN FOLLOWING

And Germany produced them, although Germany usually repudiated them. For this must also be said of the great 'German culture.' It has existed since the migration of peoples, since Christianity infiltrated the Germanic tribes. But it exists in peaks, in strata, in esoteric circles. It has never penetrated deeply into the masses of the people. There is no body of German poetry, for instance, as familiar to the whole German people as the body of English poetry is familiar to the English. German culture — except for music — especially the culture of literature and ideas, has bound itself with the German history and character only in a fragmentary manner.

And the varied history of Germany has produced many 'cultures': a monastic culture, dating from the First Reich; a court culture, grown up around the courts of great and small princes; a chivalric culture, with roots in the Middle Ages; and a modern bourgeois culture, with roots in all of them. One thing is, as I have said, characteristic of it as a whole — the urge to infinity, endless fantasy and imagination, that is without adequate form to contain it. It is, like German geography, frontierless.

Germany is the land of the unrecognized genius — the land of the prophet without a country. If the German masses follow a prophet, he is invariably a phony. A nation that produced Goethe, Hoelderlin, and Kleist takes to its bosom a charlatan like Hitler, and listens enraptured to his philosophical maunderings and 'artistic' judgments.

The sense of a great philosophic culture demands of the Leader only that he pretend to be a philosopher and the would-be founder of a great system.

Goethe and Nietzsche and many others complained bitterly that they were better understood everywhere else than in Germany. The tendency of German genius to live abroad is notorious.

The case of Bach and Haendel is representative. Born in the same year, and springing from almost identical influences — organ music, church music, and Protestantism — Haendel went to England, became court conductor, wrote coronation festivals and the great oratorios of the Church of England, won international fame, and was buried with court honors.

Bach, with his many children, his financial cares, and his intimately present God, remained in Germany, honored only by a small circle of real musicians; on the one occasion when he had court protection — that of the Kurfurst of Brandenburg — the music which he wrote and dedicated to his prince was laid away in portfolios, to be recognized for its greatness long after he had died unnoted and unmourned by more than a handful of people.

German intellectual culture has probably influenced the world more than it has influenced Germany. The ordinary German thinks of his culture as of 'the soul,' the expression of emotional imagination, metaphysical passion, a spiritual way of life or 'realm' of life, in constant contrast with reality. It is this that makes it possible for Germans to be 'carried away' — by genuine religion or by fakers.

Characteristic of German culture is its explosive tendency, its drive to shatter forms, to try to enlarge and reshape life. German genius fringes on insanity; even Goethe was, in his youth, a man of prodigious excesses that nearly killed him. His are the words, 'Rolling the eye in *fair* insanity.' Thus the German poet sees himself. Thus Hitler, emulating this concept of genius, sees himself.

This recklessness amalgamates extraordinarily with the utmost material discipline, 'workmanlike precision.' The German soldier is a remarkable phenomenon. Carrying out the most reckless orders, dictated in his mind by a High Creative Power — whether of Darkness or Light — he also

arms himself with a Baedeker and respectfully visits every
famous church and museum in the occupied countries,
including those he has bombed to hell 'in the course of
military action.'

GERMAN SPIRITUALITY

Yet there is a profound German spirituality which has to
be invoked to secure popular allegiance to any cause. Hitler
is only able to put on his campaign of conquest 'in the service of a New Order.' National Socialism is forced to mask
its real features in an appeal to the higher nature of the
German as well as to his lower nature. Aggressive militarism in Germany must be sublimated and spiritualized by
presenting it as the composite of the 'soldierly' virtues —
discipline, bravery, and absolute disregard of self. Not a
dastardly deed but is accompanied by a personal selflessness
and indifference to danger and death that are, in themselves, admirable in the extreme.

Like German science and rationalism, one can only regret
that the positive spiritual qualities of the German people are
used for such spirit-defeating ends.

But to deny German spirituality, to paint the German
as pure beast of prey, one must pass over some of the
world's greatest Christian mystics — the Germans Ekke-
hard, Tauler, Suso, Mechtild, Veit Stoss, Pacher, and
Mathias Gruenewald, the latter the artist who gave one of
the most powerful expressions in painting to the Christian
imagination.

And there were the reformers — 'the lark of Freedom,' Ulrich von Hutten, and Luther, the world's most *vehement* expression of pure and absolute religiosity.

German religious culture is not nationalist, but Christian-European, with a definite German imprint. It has found its expression in the sculpture and cathedrals of Germany. Again, the expression is exaggerated. German Gothic churches are not the most lovely in the world, but they are the most colossal. Whereas the baroque of the Latin countries, florid as it is, is yet restrained by temperateness, the German baroque is an outbreak.

In the twenties of this century the modern artistic *isms* — Dadaism, Expressionism, Sur-realism, the New Realism — whether in letters or in painting, found their wildest expression in Germany and were met in an equally exaggerated manner by Hitler, with his New Chromoism.

Fervor is a mark of the German temperament at its highest — fervor and ardor — as we see that temperament expressed in German art. Losing its purity, it degenerates into intoxication. It was the German Nietzsche, a twisted ardent spirit himself, who wrote:

> The Germans are always so badly deceived because they try to find a deceiver. If only they have a heady wine for the senses, they will put up with bad bread. *Intoxication means more to them than nourishment. That is the hook they will always bite on.* A popular leader must hold up before them the prospect of conquests and splendor; then he will be believed. They always obey and will do more than obey, provided they can get intoxicated in the process.

But Nietzsche's bitter words, which certainly modern
history has not confounded, are only partly true, seen in a
longer perspective. The German can be as fervent for
righteousness as for evil; as fervent for union with God as
for service to conquest. Perhaps the only elementary and
passionate peoples' revolution in German history was the
religiously inspired peasant rising in the time of the Refor-
mation, and it had Christian-Communistic conceptions. Its
apostle was Thomas Muenzer, mystic, frenetic, and glowing.
Like all the really popular German revolts, it was suppressed by the higher powers.

THE RELEASE INTO MUSIC

The German temperament and genius find their greatest
expression in the most unrestrained and universal of artistic
mediums — music. Here the German mind and soul cut
loose and soar. Here the eternal struggle of the German
spirit to take the universe into itself and release it again with
the mark of its own imprint succeeds in unmatchable
grandeur. Here the thesis — antithesis — synthesis: point
— counter-point are resolved in harmony.

'My kingdom is the air,' cried Beethoven, and he was not
thinking of a *Luftwaffe*. Do we not call the oppressed to rise
to Victory today with the opening bars of the Fifth Sym-
phony, written by the man who, when all Europe was falling
under the heel of Napoleon, was Europe's Other King —
free of any prejudice of nation, taking his hat off, in Whit-

man's words, 'to no man living or dead,' tearing up the dedication of the *Eroica* when Napoleon put a crown on his head, singing out of his deafness and loneliness, illness and poverty, a triumphant Hymn to Joy, and invoking a universe, an earth not made with hands, eternal in the heavens?

If, then, the Great Culture of Germany is not national but universal, and not materialistic but idealistic, what shall we say of the 'small culture,' which has given Germany her distinctive cultural personality?

THE GERMAN 'SMALL CULTURE'

That 'small culture' is also not national, in the sense that French or English culture is. It grew out of many Germanies, not one, and around many capitals, not one. Initiated by the numerous courts, it was afterward supported by the enlightened German middle classes, who kept its aristocratic quality and resisted its commercialization. Again German culture resisted materialism.

This is the culture expressed in symphonies and theaters indigenous to even the smaller cities, with first-rate instrumentalists, great choruses, and fine actors, conducted or directed by well-paid and respected artists, with the status of high civil servants.

This is the culture of the *Hausmusik*, of the innumerable amateur trios and quartets, playing together in each other's homes.

This is the culture which, previous to Hitler, maintained

the exceptional scholastic standards of even smaller universities like Heidelberg and Bonn.

In so far as this culture had ideological roots — apart from banishing Jewish composers, like Mendelssohn and Mahler — the Nazis can hardly hit at music; all this cultural life, based previously on complete intellectual and spiritual freedom, has been turned upside down by the Nazis.

But it is impossible to believe that in ten years or fifty it can be absolutely destroyed, root and branch. Darkened, yes, oppressed, confused, and scattered. But it is something that has grown up so organically, through so many political forms, over so many centuries — grown like the vegetation of the earth and not like Hitler's sown dragons' teeth — that it must live on, if only in the subconscious German mind; live on in the subconscious of even Hitler's indoctrinated generation, who have seen it only in its degeneration and destruction. Nothing is harder to destroy than cultural memory.

There are many indications in Germany, as in Italy, that among the younger generation of German students, boys and girls trained by the Hitler Youth, there is a spiritual and intellectual longing and thirst. It has not brought them to rebellion, or even to opposition to the war. But it has brought them to continuous resistance against Nazi limitations on knowledge and thought. It leads them, for instance, to look for editions of German classics unexpurgated by the Nazis.

THE 'FOLK' CULTURE

Finally, there is the 'folk' culture — the culture of the people that produced the passion plays, the village religious festivals, the fairy stories, the folk-songs, the folk-dress, the home rituals — the accumulations of thousands of years of the people's faith and wisdom. The roots of this folk culture are in the Christian ethos ... the continuity of the family; the Stable of Bethlehem, the birth of the Prince in the Manger — these are the popular legends, as the German Christmas is full of social and even revolutionary piety.

It would take Hitlerism, not decades, but hundreds of years thoroughly to uproot and destroy instincts so deeply rooted and embodied in so many simple rituals and manifestations.

And it is worthy of the greatest consideration that, not the democratic and socialistic political parties and their materialistic ideologies have most stubbornly resisted the totality of Hitlerism, but the Christian churches and the Christian ethos. For ideologies come and go in the dynamics of German intellectualism — the intellectualism which could produce both Marx and the strongest counter-revolution against him to date — but the rituals of the life of the people, the mysteries of birth and death and life expressed in those rituals, withstand, in a manner however dumb, the new intellectualism of paganism and rationalization of conquest.

It is even significant that the Nazis felt that they had to

invent a new 'Germanic' and pagan religion to accompany their political and military activities. For the Nazis know that the Germans are 'believers.' They are a people who must have a faith. They are not agnostic, even in their rationalism. Their deductive thinking indicates it. They move from intuition to knowledge, rather than from fact to conclusion. They are followers after God or after false gods, and German history, including that of the last twenty years, is strewn with little Fuehrers and way-openers, who have tried to lead the German people under one messianism or another. Hitler was the Messiah of a German world that had lost its moorings, gone through a series of terrible psychological shocks, and was ready to go crazy after 'Truth' one way or another.

Our object in this little reconnaissance raid on the German mind as revealed in its culture is, of course, neither to praise nor blame it, but to see by what roads it might be invaded.

A FEW CONCLUSIONS

The picture of idealism and universal urge, the constant presence of a tendency to erect grandiose systems, and the perennial rejection of the bread-and-butter motive by the German mind, should warn us against attempting to tempt the Germans by any small or purely materialistic solutions to large problems.

Hitler's power with the Germans may be partly attrib-

uted to the grandiosity of his aims — the grandiosity, to be
sure, of a man who is fundamentally a charlatan, not a fervent soul, but a self-intoxicated one; and not the product,
either, of German culture, but of half-education.

(If so many non-Germans did not think that a lot of
everything, even a lot of nonsense, is a sign of genius, it
would be easier to lick Hitler.)

If and when the German mind revolts from Hitler, it is
not likely to revolt in any little way, whether the revolt be
bloody or not. There may be a transitory period of exhaustion; if the war goes on long enough, we may see a frightful
intellectual and spiritual exhaustion everywhere. It can
only be hoped that it will go on long enough, however, to
see an immense intellectual and spiritual awakening in our
own world, where it is also desperately necessary.

But the German mind, if its culture reveals its tendencies,
as it must, is more likely after such an experience to go out
for a Great Solution along the lines of the most absolute
purity and repentance — for a European and world solution for peace, and for the mutual protection of our common
civilization. The opposite spirit to that of Hitler is the
spirit of Kant and Kleist, and not the spirit of 'collective
bargaining.'

The German mind is *daemonic*. Daemonic and dynamic.
In this it is infinitely nearer the Russian mind than to any
other. Nowhere outside Russia has Dostoevski had so many
readers as in Germany. The German is an economic organ-

izer, but he is not an economic man. To appeal to him to
overthrow Hitler because of three meals a day, and to
preach to him about a High Standard of Living on the basis
of the economics of either Adam Smith or Karl Marx, is to
misunderstand him and run afoul of his whole nature.

The collapse in 1918 came about because of acute hunger,
the suffering of the women and children behind the lines,
military exhaustion, and the influence of Woodrow Wilson's
Fourteen Points for an armistice. Hunger is not likely to
overcome Germany in this war. Complete military defeat
would be the most salutary thing that could happen to her,
and the greatest contribution to German education, provided military defeat can immediately open the gate to a
new rational idealism. Wilson's Fourteen Points must be
expanded, not contracted, in order to appeal to the German
mind. The epoch of self-determination and independence
must be widened to the reality and ideal of interdependence.

And, above all, our political warfare to Germany should
not be in the hands of philosophical materialists and those
who believe in the sole determinism of economics in this
world — if we wish to find allies in the German mind.
Although there were more organized followers of Marx in
Germany than in any other western country — and Marx
in his greatest purity is materialism elevated into an ideal
far beyond the commercial or the trade-union bargaining
spirit — yet these very Marxians were a pushover for Hitler appealing in the most perverted manner to German
idealism.

A daemonic mind has its devil and its angel. It was a German who created the figure of Faust. Neither angels nor devils are petty bargainers.

The opposite spirit to the spirit of paganism is the ethos of Christianity: it is not a cheap utilitarianism. And the spirit of German Christianity, as expressed through German Christian culture, is not a namby-pamby pity-the-poor sort of social-settlement Christianity, but a mortal struggle of the human soul with the evil in itself, a longing to share in the creativeness of God or perish like Lucifer. And in the folk it is a sense for the mystery of life and growth, birth and death.

The German is a destroyer or a creator. His soul moves between two polarities. He is either very very good, or very very bad. He is either, like Nietzsche, the Iconoclast, or, like Kant, the creator of an ideal system.

The German is susceptible to appeals to will, emotion, and imagination more than to appeals to intellectualism and logic. After all, it was a German Schopenhauer, who could construct a philosophical system, 'The World as *Will* and *Imagination*.'

Nothing easy and nothing unimaginative ever moves the German. The Bourgeois Revolution of the eighteenth century left very little mark on Germany. The last war and Hitler have destroyed what middle-class civilization in the French and American sense ever existed, and, as we shall see from a study of Germany's social structure, it was never the dominant civilization of Germany, even for a few decades.

Few middle-class ideas, materialistic and utilitarian, are vital in the German mind. It is futile to use them in appealing to Germany, because the German mind has rejected them consistently throughout its history, and is farther than ever from them today. The German Youth Movement revolted from them before the last war, they failed to capture the German imagination in the Republic, and Naziism has destroyed them utterly.

The German mind needs the discipline of contact with the more form-making French and Latin minds and the more realistic and practical mind of the Anglo-Saxons. But how much do we need the collaboration of the German angel to help us defeat the German devil! And how much do we need the universalism of the Germans to help us construct a new order, not of German domination, but for a commonwealth of mankind!

That is the tragedy of our western civilization.

VI

SOME NOTES ON THE SOCIAL STRUCTURE
OF GERMANY

AT THE OUTSET of this essay, which seeks to compress far too much into far too little space, I remarked that the mind of a nation is also revealed in its social structure.

The social structure of Germany, therefore, requires observation.

The Nazi Revolution has been an enormous liquidator of former German vested interests and an enormous leveler of social classes, especially of social classes regarded as *economic* groupings.

Although it first presented itself to the German people as the savior and restorer of the middle classes, with an economic program essentially populist in nature, calling for the nationalization of the great trusts, the liquidation of great merchandising concerns and the restoration of small independent business, it could not halt the economic trends of the times. Industrially, it has led to increased monopolistic state capitalism. In agriculture, it has maintained both great and small estates.

What it did restore to the urban middle classes, however, was a sense of their prestige as the chief supporters of the

Fuehrer. And a new middle class has been created by the Party, of minor bureaucrats and Gauleiters.

On these people with middle-class origins and essentially middle-class *Bildung* — Education, which must not be confused with culture — the Nazi Revolution really rests. They are the people who must, for their own self-respect, have someone under them to despise, who count the silver teaspoons and the towels and sheets in the linen closet, and are most susceptible to the myths that make them racially a master folk.

The German middle class never, historically, enjoyed the prestige and power that the American middle class has. The American middle class, like the French, created the nation. Germany, as a nation, was the creation of a military aristocracy.

After the war, defeat and inflation proletarianized the already psychologically insecure middle classes with bitter psychotic reactions. They were crushed between the organized workers and the upper classes of Junkers, big industrialists, and high-placed civil servants.

They are the most fervently nationalist of any section of German society, for they have never enjoyed either the international connections of the aristocracy or the international sympathies of the workers. They are largely the product of the German high schools, rather than the higher learning of the universities.

Every single Nazi leader comes out of this class, from

Hitler, who was the son of a petty bureaucrat, depressed into the *Lumpenproletariat* of the Vienna flophouses, raging always that he, a man of superior class, should have to share the fate of the poorest worker, through Himmler, Hess, Darré, Funk, and all the rest, not even excepting Goering and the overwhelming majority of the S.S. 'élite guards.' The German aristocrat went into the Reichswehr, not the S.S., and always despised the S.A.

The German middle class as a mentality is the hardest, therefore, to reach or influence, because its psychology is most closely bound up with that of the Nazi régime.

The German upper classes have as a whole a different mentality. They wish to win the war, and conquer large portions of the earth. But they then wish to integrate that greatly enlarged and more powerful Reich into a European society essentially aristocratic and reactionary.

They are high officers in the Army, especially officers who are hold-overs from the old régime; they are directors on the boards of great industries, who have managed to reconcile their interests with that of a powerful Nazi state, and have never become wholly imprisoned by that state; they are the big landowners whose property has never been broken up, as Hitler said it would be, into peasant small-holds. He is conquering such small-holds from non-Germanic peasants, and even conquering new estates for the old aristocracy and the new one created out of the middle classes by his 'élite guards.'

The German worker, however, is psychologically a somewhat different proposition. In the first place, neither the German *Bildung* nor the German *Kultur* has influenced him very deeply. He has been spared the high-school teachers of Germany, who were among the worst rationalizers of Hitler's mental confusions.

The German worker is a German, and therefore not completely materialistic. But he is more realistic than most members of other classes. And he has never been able to nourish himself on half-digested ideas. The New Aristocracy of profiteers from Naziism is not recruited from his ranks. The S.S. is a middle-class troop. The partly proletarian S.A. has been sidetracked since June 30, 1934.

The tangible thing in Naziism that appealed to the German worker was the end of unemployment — the fact that Hitler's state gave him a job.

But this must not be underestimated. Hitler's original followers were made of the following groups: frustrated and fearful middle classes; youth; and unemployed workers, who were either Communists or Nazis.

If the German Republic in the memory of the middle class is guilty of one thing, it is the inflation; and if in the memory of the worker it is guilty of one thing, it is the terrible period of unemployment.

In fact, it is utterly useless to try to influence the German mind to accept again as democracy the kind of party squabbling and economically anarchic republic that they had in 1918. One can only direct it to a quite different future.

The education of the worker before the Hitler régime was carried out, not by the public schools, but by the trade unions, the labor press, the labor theaters, the Consumers' Cooperatives, and the Marxian parties.

That the results of this education have by no means been obliterated from the German workers' minds is proved by every speech of Hitler, and especially by the speeches of Ley, who knows that to hold the workers you have to talk socialism, and prove that Naziism is it. The main Nazi slogan of this war, as far as the workers are concerned, is 'the war against the pluto-democracies' and 'British Imperialism,' and even in attacking Russian bolshevism, the party propagandists always couple it with 'and against pluto-democracy.'

The German industrial worker is less nationalist than the middle classes. He is interested in having steady work and a status in society. He is one of the most literate workers in Europe, and he is a thinking man. One trouble with allied political warfare is that it is conducted by people who do not know the German 'proletariat.' And most foreign offices are politically illiterate in the modern world, because they do not understand the psychology of the masses of the people, in their own countries or elsewhere.

Yet it is sure that among the listeners to foreign broadcasts there are more German workers than members of any other class. The German worker is a shrewd technician. He knows how to rebuild his radio set, and he has access to the materials with which to do so. The factory worker belongs to an organized group by the very nature of his work. Even if all independent workers' organizations are destroyed, the factory exists and is an organization. So in every factory there are, we know, some workers who listen systematically to foreign broadcasts and tell their comrades what they have heard.

Now, I have spoken of the skepticism of the German mind — combined with its opposite, the need for a Faith. Skepticism is strongest of all among the workers. They literally believe nothing they hear unless it appeals to their sense of logic. All the jokes that have percolated out of Germany — the good, sarcastic, ironic jokes — are jokes of workers. They are jokes in the dialect and the slang of the worker.

We have many proofs that the German worker is still anti-Nazi.

In prison camps, the worker-soldiers have a quite different attitude toward the war from that of the Nazi youth or the conservative officers.

And we know, from those who have escaped from German prison camps, that they did so mainly through the help of German 'common people.'

Therefore, the largest section of German society that can perhaps be influenced as a section is the so-called 'proletariat.' But how shall we influence them?

him about our 'High Standard of Living' can easily underline the Nazi propaganda about 'plutocracy.' Anyhow, the
German worker is looking for peace and security, not
riches.

A normal life is not compatible with the race theory.
Germans have always intermarried, like all other Europeans. There has always been a latent anti-Semitism —
more virulent among peasants than townsmen and worse in
Catholic Germany, including Austria, than in Protestant.
It has been terribly enhanced by propaganda turning the
Jew into a bogey. But the general restrictions on marriage,
the search after grandparents, and the new experiments in
breeding a 'superior race' are unpopular and seem utterly
foolish to the average man.

A normal life does not mean paganism. The working
classes are the least religious of any in Germany, but they
are by no means the least ethical, and they are certainly not
paganists. Christianity has been one of the most profound
molding forces of the German and the European mind.

A normal life is not a life of revenge. Revenge and fear
of revenge distress not only the Germans but all European
peoples. The sufferings of the common people in Germany
and all Europe are almost beyond the power of imagination,
and they are too absent from our minds most of the time.
A bleak resignation is over Europe — that violence and
chaos and destruction may go on interminably. And the
German fear of revenge is Hitler's greatest asset at this stage

of the war. 'If we don't win, we will be exterminated,' is an idea that is constantly played upon by Goebbels, and under no circumstances should it be underlined. Punishments must be promised to certain guilty leaders, a threat to which the German mind is by no means completely opposed.[1] The Gestapo, for instance, is not the White-Headed Boy of the German people.

A normal life for Europe is not a life of wild and unrestricted nationalism as some of our own most chauvinistic statesmen seem to believe. Extreme nationalism is a characteristic of politicians and monopolists who profiteer on it, not of peoples. Europeans never believed that the economic frontiers crisscrossing Europe make sense, and all Europeans have suffered indescribable inconveniences from them. The European peoples do not, normally, hate each other. And exaggerated nationalism has a very recent history.

There was completely free movement of peoples in Europe up until the First World War, with the exception of Russia and Turkey. A normal life for Europe is a life of distinct nations living in friendship without exaggerated barriers between them. At this moment Switzerland is perhaps the most representative state in Europe of what Europeans consider normal — and not the least so.

A normal life for a German as a European is a life of cultural autonomy, a life of distinct national languages, lit-

[1] Since this was written, President Roosevelt has made his statement that post-war punishments will be confined to responsible criminals, and has been backed up by the leaders of Britain and the Soviet Union.

eratures, and arts, not in the least irreconcilable with non-national economic and political adjustments.

It is not a uniform or cosmopolitan life. The popular rejection of communism was due rather to its cosmopolitan characteristics, its contempt for cultural traditions, than to its socialism.

If one thinks of peace in such popular terms, then one can talk to Germans. If one speaks in technical and juridical terms, one will encounter pure skepticism.

The more one is able to put oneself in the place of one's enemy as a fellow sufferer from the nonsenses and evils which oppress the whole world, the more likely one is to penetrate through to him.

Finally, the modern non-Nazi German, especially the worker, has serious doubts about all existing governments. The German adult has never once lived under a government that he liked or that succeeded. The Kaiserreich fell; the Republic was weak; the Hitler Reich took him to war. Hitler's propaganda has made him doubt whether any other governments are much better.

The less, therefore, that government spokesmen speak or write to Germany, and the more the German is approached by unofficial and forthright people who share some of his own apprehensions and disgust about the world we live in, the more direct will be the communication.

And this is the more true, because the German, worker or otherwise, cannot be 'sold' on the idea that America is a

Utopia. He knows too much about us for that. And, indeed, the question of how the German mind sees *us* is also pertinent to a survey of the German's mental defenses. Let us consider his opinion, because, whether we like it or not, it is part of the mental fortress that we wish to break down.

VII

The Grapes of Wrath was a best-seller in Fascist Italy, and for all I know in Germany as well. (I hope Mr. Steinbeck got his royalties.) It is true that Ignacio Silone's *Fontamara* and *Bread and Wine*, which are the Grapes of Wrath of contemporary Italian literature, had to be written in Switzerland, and could not be published in Italy or Germany, and it is also true that the Italian and German people are in greater or less degree disillusioned with their own social and economic system, especially since the war.

But that does not make them admire ours.

The Germans, like the Italians, know little about our history and our political and economic institutions, and what they know about the latter is not very impressive to them.

The German view of our society has been largely influenced by Hollywood films, by American novels of the twenties, and by the descriptions of Doctor Goebbels. Our films, which had wide circulation in Germany before Hitler, systematically portrayed America as an exclusively middle-class nation — it is rare that one saw a workman, or a workman's drama, or a farmer on a Hollywood film. The life and standards portrayed by Hollywood seem to Germans to belong to a non-existent or long-forgotten world It is a world that suggests nothing to them as a picture of reconstruction.

Adult Germans who read foreign books formed their strongest picture of us from the iconoclastic literature of the twenties depicting America in a sharp and cruel light. Upton Sinclair and Sinclair Lewis were best-sellers throughout the whole post-war period. The American writer who had the greatest appeal to German youth, however, was a writer with a profound affirmative idealism, spirituality, and titanism: Thomas Wolfe.

The average German knows that we are very rich, but he also knows that until we began active war production we had a long period of dreadful unemployment, and 'poverty in the midst of plenty.'

The German worker fears unemployment more than anything on earth, and perhaps more than anyone else on earth, since work to him is more than income, but his greatest pride. He thanks his Fuehrer for work, and thinks little about the fact that war preparations gave him his work, too, only earlier.

He is not interested in our elections, which he suspects — judging from his own experience under the Republic — are manipulated by machines, with candidates selected for their party reliability or their subservience to powerful economic or group interests. And he believes American politics are full of crime and gangsterism.

He believes that we are a plutocratic country, ruled for the most part by Big Business. He conceives of our business as a gross commercialism hampering the most reasonable use of our capacities.

On the other hand, he has great respect for the American as a type. He thinks Americans are all tall, athletic, and full of courage and energy. He is impressed with Americans as sportsmen. Adult Germans who fought in the last war remember fully the appearance of the Americans on the western front — the sheer physical impression that they made.

He admires the largeness of America and its absence of internal frontiers. He is envious of our lack of militarism, which the common German loves much less than our 'intellectuals' believe.

He conceives us to be a people happily free from the personal interferences of officious bureaucrats,[1] and exempt from the pryings of the police state.

He believes America to be a country of the future. And he has no doubts whatever about our industrial plant and capacity. He knows that the rationalization of German industry was laid out on American mass-production lines.

Despite our commercialism, he suspects (and correctly) that we are, at bedrock base, a nation of idealists.

He believes in our good intentions, as a people. He remembers that America did not sign the Treaty of Versailles, and *did*

[1] In this he is mistaken — alas!

feed German children after the last war. He thinks we are disinterested in Europe, and less than the British afraid of German competition.

On the other hand, he exaggerates our labor troubles, which have been played up continually by the German propaganda, and he also exaggerates racial cleavages, convinced that Germans and Italians in America are all on the side of the Axis.

Any attempt to 'sell' our society to Germany (or to any other country) as a sort of earthly Paradise will run up against a disgusted attitude that will immediately brand it as 'pure propaganda.'

On the other hand, much can be done to break down some fixed ideas and prejudices.

Every theoretical and practical contribution of labor to a more effective war effort should be played up in our propaganda, and preferably by spokesmen for the workers themselves, instead of officials or professional radio announcers.

A manifesto signed by a half million Americans of German origin, calling on German workers to stop this fratricidal war, get rid of Hitler, and work with them for a new world, would be a half million times more effective than the President of the United States giving such advice. For it would contribute to dispel the theory that all German-Americans are on the German side.

And the less we try to sell ourselves as a heaven on earth, and the more openly we admit that we are full of faults, but nevertheless are intellectually and spiritually free and determined to create a better world, the more convincing and disarming we shall be, especially if we plead for help in it.

But above all, our political warfare must be lifted out of the realm of conventional propaganda, put on by news announcers and dramatized by Hollywood 'experts,' and it must revolve continually and consistently around basic principles for the establishment of peace and security, freedom and equality, on this earth.

For there is one thing in which the German mind is *not* divided.

There is one thing in which it is no different from any other mind.

The German people want peace.

All the peoples of the earth want peace. The ability to frame principles for a peace acceptable to the rational mind and the yearnings of the human spirit is the greatest political weapon of this war and the one most calculated to blast down the Verduns in the German mind.

It is ironic that Americans do not see that a true description of the purposes of a new world is written in the preamble to their own Constitution:

'In order to form a more perfect union, establish justice, insure domestic tranquillity, provide for the common defense, promote the general welfare, and secure the blessings of liberty to ourselves and to posterity.'

VIII

THE PASSION FOR PEACE

THE DESIRE FOR PEACE is the uppermost passion in the minds of all peoples and the source of the deepest troubling of the spirit of man. There is a universal sense of guilt about this war, common to Germans and everyone else. That each tries to assess the entire guilt to the others is only evidence of the *common* sense of guilt. There is a universal feeling that all have sinned, whether by direct and terrible aggression, or whether indirectly by the chase after comfort and money, and the failure to comprehend what is a literal truth — that men *are* their brothers' keepers.

And there is a universal apprehension, from which not a single nation is free, that if this war goes on indefinitely, it will destroy civilization itself and leave mankind dazed and exhausted upon a shattered planet.

Why, in God's name, should we not turn this passion for peace, in full admission of all our own shortcomings, into our greatest instrument? Can we not ask ourselves the questions put by Kleist, and answer them in as noble a manner? Are we fighting for anything on earth except the freedom of our own nation and the freedom of all nations, in order out of this freedom to construct at long last a world in harmony with man's long-neglected Reason and Conscience?

HITLER AND THE PEACE YEARNING

That the thirst for peace is today the deepest passion of the German soul is revealed in all of Hitler's wartime speeches. He conducts a constant apology for this war. He washes his hands of its guilt in every speech to the German nation. He insists that the date of the outbreak of the war be shoved ahead two days, and starts it, not from the attack on Poland, but from the British declaration of the fact that a 'state of war exists.'

This British statement is never passed over by German propagandists.

They do not, of course, tell an accurate story. They do not recall that Britain's entrance into the war came about as the result of a repeated, publicly stated intention to recognize her treaty obligations after Hitler had flagrantly broken a publicly given word, and that even after German troops were marching into Poland, Britain waited for two full days, while the Polish Ambassador stood ready to resume negotiations.

We have given aid and comfort to the enemy, of inestimable value to him in maintaining his home morale, by the treasonable talk of opposition elements at home, suggesting that it is we, the democracies, instead of the Fascist imperialist powers and their friends in the democracies, who precipitated this war.

Our fault lies, not in our action, but in our inaction. It lies in failure to realize that what was happening inside Germany, domestically, concerned us.

Hitler's war was meticulously prepared for. And never for a day should we interrupt a constant accusation of guilt against its instigators, while admitting our own criminal blindness and smugness.

For if there were no latent feeling of guilt in the German mind, Hitler would not be at such pains to remove it. If there were no passionate desire for peace in Germany, despite all the victories, Hitler would not, as he constantly does, accuse his enemies of plotting the war. This attempt to make a transference of responsibility is one of the most interesting symptoms of another cleavage in the German mind.

For, historically, German statesmen have never thought that war for national aims was anything to apologize for — even aggressive war. In the last war, German swords carried the insignia in Latin, 'The ultimate appeal to reason.' German thinkers and writers, calling themselves 'realists,' maintained that war was a natural order of affairs upon this planet, and that a great nation, needful or desirous of expansion and power, was justified in using its talents aggressively to realize its aims.

No one in German history more unhesitatingly advanced this theory than Hitler himself. 'The sword must conquer land for German ploughshares.' 'No alliance is worth anything unless its purpose is war.'

Quotation could be piled upon quotation to prove that, previous to the intensification of international relations, Hitler felt not the slightest need to apologize for war as the instrument for fulfilling national purposes or appetites.

But the enthusiasm with which the Munich Pact and later the Russian Pact were hailed in Germany, as well as in London and Paris, must have given him some pause.

So here we strike a cleavage even in the mind of Hitler himself. He knows the war is unpopular; he feels it absolutely essential to remove its guilt from his person. Yet, at the same time, he is the prisoner of his own demands for *Lebensraum*, which cannot possibly be reconciled with a purely defensive war against malicious attackers. He tries to find a way out by pinning the guilt on Britain for interfering with 'natural German living space' — living space that, Britain or no Britain, could not be acquired without aggression. The attack on Russia has to be explained as the forestalling of a planned Russian attack on Germany, and this attack he has been least able to explain at all.

When Hitler tries to explain the causes of the war and the purposes of the war, he therefore contradicts himself. One moment he is conquering *Lebensraum* in the East; the next he is protecting European civilization against 'Bolshevist hordes' — a thousand miles inside Russia; the next he is anti-imperialist, and defending freedom for India — thoroughly hypocritical from a man who in *Mein Kampf* had nothing but words of praise for British imperialist policy, except that it was too weak.

And a note repeatedly occurs in the German home propaganda: 'We are no worse than anyone else — they are all hypocrites.'

In this situation two countries have the greatest potential power over the German mind: the United States and Russia. For the Germans do not believe that either Russians or Americans are imperialists. And whatever they think of themselves, they do know that Japan is imperialist — and, incidentally, there is a long, long history of anti-Japanese writings and teachings in the German mind. 'The Yellow Peril' is a German idea — as well as an American idea. And the Yellow Peril in the German mind is the aggressive nationalism of Japan; it was not based originally on racial prejudice, though Hitler has greatly increased racial prejudice, but on the fear that the more numerous colored races of Asia might one day attack the white world under Japanese leadership, and in a spirit of utmost revenge.

The confusion, therefore, in the German mind and in Hitler's mind about the issues of this war must be immense. For we should never forget that the war that came was not the one Hitler wanted. He wanted an alliance with Britain, or Britain's benevolent neutrality against Russia. And the Chamberlain Government certainly encouraged him to think he could get it. He wanted that in *Mein Kampf*, he wanted it at Munich, he wanted it after Poland, and he wanted it in May, 1941, when Hess flew to England.

Failing that, he wanted an alliance with Russia against Britain. He tried to get it before attacking Russia, but could only get doubtful neutrality and a recognition of certain Russian interests in eastern Europe.

The Japanese are profoundly unpopular in Germany, and Hitler would like to have had a war he could fight without them. But to defeat Britain and cripple America he needed Japanese aid, and the Japanese seized opportunity. Germany knows that the Japanese, and not the German Reich, are becoming the heirs to Europe's Asiatic colonies, and that Japanese militarists hate the white world about equally.

All these confusions need to be exploited by our propaganda, through the most trenchant analysis. Political warfare should never argue. It should raise questions and pronounce judgment. Why did Hitler declare war on the United States? Why did Hitler have to spring to the defense of Japan against North America, in which live millions of men of German blood? What conceivable gain for Germany can grow out of Japanese victories in the Far East?

At the same time, the feeling of German guilt should be raised by recounting in detail the prelude to this war, and every well-founded atrocity committed by the Nazis in Europe. The wholesale movements of populations should be condemned, and on the most straightforward grounds. It should be presumed that hundreds of thousands of Germans share our horror at such things, but they should be warned that unless they are able to influence their Government, the world will be inclined to hold them all responsible. They should be encouraged to devise means to establish their personal innocence and protect themselves against any future charge of complicity.

*And at all times we should be the advocates of peace. We should
wage an unremitting peace offensive.*

But in order to do so, we must have clear principles for a
peace. Any peace that will appeal to energetic German
and European minds must mean the reorganization of the
world, and especially of the western world to which we belong, on principles acceptable to reasonable men in any nation, enemy or ally; principles in the framework of which all
peoples can see a future in which they can live in equality
with the fullest use of their talents and skills and without the
inheritance of revenge.

At the risk of indulging in boring repetition, the greatest
single propaganda asset that Hitler has today is the fear he
is able to instill in his people that Germany has no choice
but to pursue this war to its ultimate conclusion, victory or
defeat. It is a simple matter of survive or perish, they are
told. 'It is the German nation that is at stake and not my
person,' says Hitler.

Hitler's other greatest asset is the doubt of the German
people that any government means what it says. They are
uninclined to trust the American Government or any other,
however much they might be brought to trust the American
people, because they remember Wilson's Fourteen Points
and what happened to them in Paris.

A guarantee given to the world by the American, British,
and Russian people — actually as people, millions of individuals, signing a manifesto — might convince them, and

would certainly impress them. But nothing coming merely from a government source. For they know enough about us to realize that governments come and go; that the pledge of one President does not commit the next, nor even the current Congress.

The formulation of positive principles accepted and recorded as the will of the American people by something like a Gallup poll is the only way to find the answer to the question: With what Germans can we make peace?

With the economic classes leveled as they have been in Germany, with all the pre-Hitler social and political institutions destroyed, as they have been, with the German mind rocked to its foundations by a quarter-century of instability and disaster culminating in this new war, we literally do not know where our German internal allies are to be found.

The truth is we will never have any until we create them.

They are there, to be created, probably more potential among the workers than elsewhere. But we might find them where we least expect them. Although we would hardly find the German Army, as an institution, our ally, we might find many among German officers and in every rank of German society as well. For Germany, like the rest of the world, is desperately unhappy. And in Germany, as everywhere else, the individual person thinks his own thoughts.

If we are appealing to the 'Common People' for the 'Century of the Common Man,' we need some new definitions.

What do we mean by the 'Common People'? Are we going in for an inverted snobbery that attributes creative power exclusively to hand-workers, or that brands every wealthy man a knave, *per se*, or that seeks to elevate the mediocre run-of-the-mill into an international ideal?

Let us define what we mean.

The 'common people' all over the world today are not to be catalogued by social or economic class. They are all those who recognize their kinship with the commonalty of mankind. They are all those who share a common suffering and yearn for a common human aim. They are all those who seek a common meaning through a common sense for the establishment of a community and a commonwealth in harmony with their reason and their consciences. The cheap concept that an industrial worker necessarily because of the grease on his hands belongs to that commonalty of men was never true. Today it is less true than ever. The Queen of England today, because of the motherliness in her heart — a motherliness full of concern and pain for the sufferings of people, all people — belongs to that new 'common people' who are common because they share commonalty.

But these 'common people' all over the world need principles around which they can rally for the establishment of a new internationalism of freedom and dignity.

Fascism has shot its bolt. As an 'ideology' it has proved incapable of rallying to itself the heart and reason of the human race. *Hitler has lost his revolution!* He has lost it long before he has lost his war, and I suspect that he knows it.

Russian communism has been constantly evolving —

evolving from rebellion to the consolidation of a socialist state — and in its own terrible bath of fire has burned away much dross. Its call to class warfare dies in the moment when the hearts of all decent men, of whatever class and creed, contract in the most acute pain at Russian sufferings; its cosmopolitanism — in contrast to internationalism — withers in the struggle for the Russian nation; its atheism is empty when prayer for deliverance comes to the soldiers' lips. There is more religious spirit in the Russian struggle than there was in the phony war of so-called Christian France. Its socialism is alive, and will remain alive.

There is a revolutionary sense in the world — without revolutionary formulation. *Revolution is not rebellion.* Rebellion is radical reaction to radical evils. But revolution, as Mazzini knew, and as Washington and Jefferson knew, is not the rebellion, but the consolidating principles that arise to introduce a new epoch. Stalin has an instinct about this, too. That is why he ruthlessly suppressed the eternal rebels with their concept of the 'perpetual' revolution. Only rebellion can be 'perpetual.'

We must create our revolutionary allies in enemy countries by creating revolutionary principles *for ourselves*, and raising a banner 'to which the wise and the just can repair.' We must create the revolution of the wise and the just.

We do not know how many Germans in Hitler's Reich would rally to such a banner. *But we never shall know until we raise it.* And when we raise it, we will find the answer to the question: With what Germans can we make peace?

For the answer is obvious: With *any* Germans who will accept the *principles and offer adequate material guarantees of fidelity to them — guarantees of fidelity equal to our own.*

The acceptance of such principles and the furnishing of guarantees rule out Hitler and the Nazis automatically. For no principles could be formulated acceptable to free men and acceptable to Naziism, and no fidelity pledged by Hitler offers any guarantee — on the record.

The Atlantic Charter is not an adequate statement of principles, and it represents no one except its authors. It leaves too many gaps; it offers too many outs; and in some particulars, notably its failure to deal with the matter of national sovereignties, it runs counter to the most dynamic thought in the modern world.

The Freedoms it offers are inadequate. They are mere verbiage. It does not tell a skeptical world how it is to be freed from 'want and fear.'

There is not the slightest good for us to promise to free the world from want and fear when the whole world knows that we have not managed to free ourselves from them, as yet. Nor can we free ourselves from them as a segment of mankind.

People want many more freedoms than the famous four. They want, as I have pointed out, freedom to move. They want guarantees of freedom from *specific* fears, such as the pryings of the police state and the pryings of arrogant and irresponsible bureaucracies. They want freedom to be in a minority, which is not assured by mere freedom of speech. *They want freedom to be creative*, to share in creating the principles and structure of the world in which they are sacrificing and dying.

They want freedom to love; freedom to bring up their children in a sensible world that recognizes some simple ethical rules about human behavior — and sees that those rules are enforced. They want *freedom from war*. They want freedom from the parasitism that burdens our economy with too many middlemen, each taking a cut out of the creative activity of the organizer and worker.

They want freedom from the overpowerful commercialism that poisons our theaters and our press, that creates 'personalities' through build-ups, and encourages waste and false standards by lying advertising.

They want freedom *in order to be free. They want a freedom in which their work, the creative expression of their lives, is not regarded as a commodity to be bought and sold like so much soap.*

They want the freedom that Jesus understood, and Jefferson understood, and Lincoln understood — the freedom, at long last, to be Men, with business and government subservient to men and not men to business and government.

There is no use in advancing to the world 'Anglo-American principles.' The principles of a good society are not racially or nationally founded. To believe so is to be already half a Nazi. To believe that Naziism is an exclusively German phenomenon is to disregard the evidence all about ourselves.

Naziism is the final logic of total nationalism that insists that there is no society to which mankind belongs and no loyalties that command his allegiance except those of the Nation. Were that idea ever accepted by a majority of Americans, our society would develop all the characteristics of Nazi Germany, differentiated in details by our cultural habits, but no less brutal and violent.

Principles for a just and lasting peace must be principles developed out of the realities of the modern world; based upon a rational analysis of its facts and needs, and rooted in the moral nature of Man. They need not be, nor should they be, a blueprint. Rome was not built in a day, and neither will the New World be. But they must be principles divorced from exclusive individual national aspirations, and they must give fullest recognition to the outstanding fact of the twentieth century and the reality revealed by this war: namely, that *the world is one single habitation for mankind and must at long last be governed. For the absence of world government is world anarchy.*

It is our failure to have basic principles to guide us that confuses us in such a matter as the India question. Let us by all means be for the freedom of India and the end of all national imperialisms. But let us not be for the total independence of India, or of any other nation. Let us not in the case of India champion a theory which the origins of this war should have exploded, once and for all — namely, that any nation, unlike any person, has the right to do anything it pleases or withhold anything it pleases, regardless of the Society of Mankind. Why do we continue to claim for ourselves or demand for others, as nations, which are mere segments of a world society, what we would not dream of claiming for ourselves as individual persons: the right to be sovereign over all law?

The question to be posed is whether the world shall be governed by one or two nations, exploiting it in their own interests, or mutually governed by all for the welfare of all. *That is the basic issue of this war.* That is the revolutionary foundation for the new World Commonwealth.

The reason why we do not pose the question is that we are ourselves divided — divided within the United Nations and divided even within the United States. We play with such concepts as 'western hemisphere policy' — to the delight of the Nazi mind, which wants nothing more than our acceptance of the 'sphere-of-influence' idea. For the German leaders are geo-politicians and know that there is no 'western hemisphere' unless we include half of the Atlantic and Pacific Oceans; that the population resources of both the Americas together are less than those of central, eastern Europe, and European Russia alone; that Latin America is more dependent culturally and economically upon Europe than upon us; and that who rules continental Europe, Eurasia, and Africa eventually rules the earth.

To the youth of America and the world it is our duty to make clear that *any outcome of this war that divides the world into monstrous superstates under various leaderships will mean another titanic conflict, and within their lifetimes.*

We must not suggest in our propaganda such Nazi ideas, which the Nazis can take up and make the basis for their own peace offensive.

And magazine and newspaper editors must be compelled, by the existence of principles, to exercise a discipline over what they print, which, getting back to Germany via neutral Latin-American countries, encourages the German people to believe that they can get a Nazi negotiated peace.

Our business is to clarify the confusions of the enemy, not confuse him further, while furnishing him with material with which to create confusions among ourselves.

IX

ON THE NEED FOR PRINCIPLES

BUT can such principles be formulated?

On September 5, 1942, a long article by Harold Callender in the *New York Times* quoted an official of the Office of War Information as follows:

> There have been few basic statements of policy. For example, the Germans are unifying Europe by force, creating a larger industrial center in Czecho-Slovakia and Poland to replace the bomb-battered Rhineland, and they promise to create still another in the Donetz Basin, linked by new roads and railways. They strive to remove whole populations, Dutch to the East, for instance, to make Europe a single economic unit under German domination. European economic unity has long been an ideal. *But what picture of a future Europe can we set up against this militarized unity taking shape in wartime, some are asking here.*[1]

The answer to that question *can be made*, but in order to make it we must recognize certain things about Europe.

Some American spokesmen are still acting as though the chief objective for which this war is being fought is the restoration of 'private enterprise,' everywhere. Mr. Hoover has the opinion that the restoration of international trade to private enterprise is a prime condition of a 'lasting peace.'

[1] Italics are *mine*.

Considering that this state of affairs existed in August, 1914, one wonders at the basis for his faith.

Those who take the viewpoint that it is necessary to create *new* international economic institutions are usually called 'Utopists' by those who believe in what is called the American System.

But it is actually they who are Utopists. They have once lived in their Utopia, *circa* 1926, before the Great Depression, and their dream is to get back to it. Their Utopia is behind them. Confronted with the realities and the needs of the present century, they are utterly without solutions.

It is quite impossible to reconstruct Europe on the basis of nineteenth-century private capitalism, and there is no will among the overwhelming majority of Europeans so to reconstruct it. The revolt against Hitlerism in the occupied countries is not a revolt against his 'socialism.' It arises from a recognition of the fact that what he has established is not socialism at all, but a monopolistic state capitalism in the interests of a 'managerial revolution' of Germanic industrial leaders and Nazi Party officials.

Germany has, as the official stated, built up huge new industries in non-Germanic countries. These industries have been financed by the German state, which now controls the entire resources of the occupied countries, and by German industrialists who have been granted shares in these state-protected industries. A few other European capitalists have been allowed to come into the combine for the sake of their capital and in order to secure their allegiance.

What, in the event of our victory, is to be done with these industries? To what private enterprisers shall they be assigned? Are Polish or Czech or Dutch capitalists to inherit them? Are American private enterprisers to obtain their shares under favorable conditions?

How can any such proposals be made to the people of Europe by us? If any such proposal were made by us, Naziism would probably promptly move economically to the left; the slogan of British-American pluto-democracy would be given the substance of truth, and the very people in Europe, above all the workers, who are the foundation of the democratic resistance, would be plunged into deepest confusion.

Just how, also, are we to restore *Russian* international trade to private enterprise? Russia has undergone great transformations in the last years and has become steadily more conservative, especially in such matters as home life, marriage, education, culture, and personal and truly private property. But Russia is a socialist state and will remain a socialist state, however much her other than economic institutions may be 'democratized.' The Russian worker, actor, engineer, or industrial manager receives wages or a salary, and may invest his surplus income, but exclusively in state bonds, for the state is the financier of all industries. He may own income and derive income from investments of his savings in the state, but he may not derive income from direct investments in productive property. And there is not the slightest prospect of this being changed except by Nazi or Japanese conquerors, who would not restore private enterprise to mythical Russian capitalists, but would take over *state* enterprise for their own purposes.

In all the countries that have been occupied by the Nazis, privately held shares in productive property have been expropriated and have passed into German hands. But they have not been expropriated without compensation, and in each case, although the sales have been forced, they have been 'legal.' This has even been done with the property of Jews, who have been expropriated without compensation only in the form of special taxes, or have been compensated at a tiny fraction of value.

But how can these legally exchanged properties be restored to their original owners, who are scattered and dead? Most of them cannot be.

Most of these properties can only be restored to the people of the nations where they are situated. We cannot hand over to Polish capitalists German properties built from Polish resources, with Polish labor, for the purpose of subjugating further the Polish population. We can only hand them over to the people of Poland — as Polish state enterprises.

Private capitalism, *as we have known it*, is a concept as dead as the proverbial dodo in most of Europe. It is dead in Germany. The only things about National Socialism which are deeply popular with the German masses are German national unity and all the semi-socialist measures which the Nazi state has introduced. The Germans want more socialism, not less.

Private capitalism in Germany after the last war was largely supported by foreign money and represented in the German mind 'bondage to foreign plutocrats.' Nobody in Germany — but literally nobody — has believed in classic capitalism since the 1923 inflation, which completely destroyed all money values.

And in the exchange of goods between nations, it is impossible to create a balanced trade, avoiding gluts and scarcities, and distributing the products essential to the life of mankind to those who are in need of them, without international institutions for the exercise of guidance and control.

In order to formulate principles to guide the establishment of a new world, we have got to take into account the present state and necessities of the world and the dynamic tendencies of the times everywhere. There are still Americans who believe in the 'natural harmony' of untrammeled economic forces, but there has been nothing in the last generation to support them in this Utopian concept. Certainly there has been nothing in Europe.

We seek to appeal to that German mind which is open to a reintegration with the rest of civilization, not as Supermen, but as Equals.

But we can only appeal to that mind in a manner and

with a program that is sensible to most Europeans and peoples.

The American people must dispel bogies from their minds. There is literally no group in the world today that wants to see anywhere a 'bolshevist' revolution, with its attendant 1918 characteristics of violence, atheism, attack on all existent institutions, and 'dictatorship of the proletariat.' Russia does not want such a revolution — obviously not during the war, but not after the war either. Stalin has spent his time as the head of the Russian socialist state attempting to consolidate the state and bring life to normal, and in the course of it has liquidated the supporters of 'permanent revolution.'

A bolshevist revolution in Europe would be upsetting to the whole evolution of Russia in the last twenty years. It would create more Trotskys.

There is no danger to the Church from the Left in any section of Protestant Europe. On the contrary, the more the Church emphasizes the basic ethical principles of Christianity as applied to society, the stronger its influence becomes. The Lord's Prayer is a prayer for *this earth*. Nor is there any danger to the Catholic Church except to such sections of it as have openly allied themselves with Fascism and tyranny. Some of the finest social thought in the world today and some of the finest thinking on the nature of Freedom are coming from Catholic philosophers.[1]

---

[1] See the Manifesto of European Catholics published in *The Commonweal*, New York, in August, 1942.

The Dictatorship of the Proletariat becomes nonsensical in a Europe where the Nazis are rapidly proletarianizing everybody except a few big capitalists who choose to cut in on the loot. The Dictatorship of the People is Democracy.

But there is a firm, quiet, intense conviction among the peoples everywhere — in China and India and England, no less than in Europe — that the resources, machines, and skills of every nation must be used for the welfare of the masses of the people of those nations; that cycles of employment and unemployment must cease; that money profits must not be the primary criterion of value; and that the surplus wealth of nations must be available to other peoples.

And unless one can affirm and describe a social, political, and economic order that bids fair to meet obvious world problems, there is only limited truth in telling the people of Germany or of Europe, or of any other place on the globe, that we are fighting for their freedom and ours.

We need to create a set of principles which admit that to a certain extent we are all in the same boat. *Our* advantage is that we can get out of the boat — and help the rest of the world out of it — without having our Fuehrer sink us when he finds out what we are up to. For though we are not free from want and fear, we do have freedom of speech and freedom of religion and freedom of intellect. We can still use our brains, without thinking and speaking ourselves behind barbed wire. Out of freedom of thought, feeling, and expression, we have to create the other freedoms, for ourselves and for the world — including the world of our enemies.

We have to think our way through to freedom — freedom for America in a free world and freedom for America in an ordered world. For there is no freedom in an anarchic world. There is only war and more war and more war.

Oswald Spengler, who was a deeply skeptical and pessimistic German, wrote: 'The Twentieth Century will be a century of Caesarism and World Wars.'

By another of those German paradoxes he renounced the Nazis, who claimed him, before he died in the middle of seeing his prophecy fulfilled.

But are *we* going to help fulfill it?

X

PRINCIPLES FOR A PEOPLES' PEACE

I BELIEVE that certain principles can be formulated which synthesize the progressive thought of the whole world at present — including the thought of an unknown but not unexistent number of Germans. These principles might, I believe, be reduced to ten. I offer them tentatively and with humility.

1) There is no solution for any single European nation which is not a European solution, and no solution for the European question which is not a solution for every European nation. We cannot abolish any nation as a fact in Europe, or deny to any one of them whatever it is willing to grant to all others.

2) There is no solution for the American, British, or Russian nations which is not, at once, a European and Far Eastern solution. Under no circumstances do we regard ourselves as an isolated hemisphere, island, or continent. We are all historically committed to the principles of Freedom and Equality, and we are determined to see their establishment as the only basis of peace.

3) We would welcome federations of states eliminating

the numbers of customs frontiers and innumerable bureaucracies. The Federal principle is a foundation of the United
States. We only insist upon full cultural autonomy for all
states, great or small, checks to prevent the political domination of small states by their larger neighbors or the economic servitude of small states to larger, and equality of
rights within any framework that may be constructed.

4) We recognize that there is a world economy which is
inextricable, and demand the creation of appropriate national and international institutions to further the productive capacities of the various nations and guide a balanced
exchange of goods between them, in order to avoid crises of
glut and scarcity, and achieve the mutual development of
this planet for the welfare of the inhabitants upon it.

5) We favor the establishment of an international banking system, mutually established and controlled, to provide
the world with a stable currency accessible to all.

6) We assert the basic equality of all peoples on this
earth, taking account of the fact that some have reached
higher stages of development than others and, therefore,
and because of this fact, owe a duty to these others. We
recognize at the same time that equality of right does not
necessarily mean identity of function, nor imply that there
are not distinct cultures that can best flourish in nationally
consolidated and relatively homogeneous communities.[1]

---

[1] We should not foster the cheap cosmopolitanism that denies the reality
or the creative power of national communities, or favors wholesale amal-
gams of races and peoples.   Neither reason nor experience justifies it.

7) We favor an international police force recruited proportionately from among all nations and peoples who join in our common effort to create a secure and reasonable world, and responsible to a superior mutually created sovereignty above us all. The right of any individual nation to make war must be as restricted as the right of any individual person to make war.

8) We favor the mandating of all colonies to a superior trusteeship, mutually created and charged to promote and execute plans for the development and colonization of backward areas, with a constant view to the interests of the native inhabitants and the general welfare of the world.

9) We favor the liberation of all nations *in the framework of these principles.*

10) No restrictions as to political forms are imposed upon any nation or federation of nations, except that all systems embody a bill of rights, guaranteeing the liberty and security of the person and free personal, intellectual, scientific, and religious intercourse within and between nations.

Such principles are in harmony with the trend of progressive thinking all over the world, in enemy countries as well as among allies.

They epitomize the world revolution for civilization, rooted in reason, realism, and morality, that must conquer the mind of this world if the war is not to be fought for 'mere survival.'

Political warfare on the highest plane is fought around daring ideas. They are still more powerful than tanks and planes. They are the only weapons with the power to *resolve* the issues of this war — and win the war by resolving them.

Without them we may enter into an interminable struggle that will leave the earth so exhausted, impoverished, and brutalized that it will take generations to restore it. Without them victory will be an armistice between wars. Without them the war may drift into aimless and undirected rebellions, arising out of sheer despair, and turning our earth into desperate and divided groups, each under petty leaders, fighting each other for bread.

Emerson said: Nothing will bring you Peace but the triumph of principle.

Peace, as the triumph of principle, is Victory.

XI

A FINAL WORD ON 'HANS'

I SHOULD LIKE to say all these things to 'Hans.' But I am a private citizen, forced to confine my talks to the framework suggested by our national leadership. It is only to my fellow citizens that I can speak as openly as I have done. My belief in my own country, in the idealism and common sense of our people, in the wisdom of our constitutional founders, in the passionate vision of our poets, in the mission for humanity implicit in this nation that embraces so many races and creeds, may not translate itself as an individual enterprise into revolutionary democracy across the world-covering ether.

When my publishers asked permission to print the following broadcasts, I demurred, feeling them, then as now, utterly inadequate — words spoken by one who has seen the ruin of London and Plymouth and Bristol, the gutted House of Commons, the lean, grim, purposeful faces of shabby Durham workers, and the brave smile of a crippled child.

Words spoken by one who can imagine the tower of Muenster falling, and six-hundred-year-old Lübeck, a gem embalming the work of long dead hands, a rubble in the dust.

Words spoken by one to whom the fight before Stalingrad, with its piled-up human sacrifice, is a pain too dry for tears.

Words spoken by one who believes with deepest conviction that out of the Great Destruction must come the Great Re-Creation, if Man is to justify his claim to being a creature made in the image of God, and higher than the animals.

And I cannot conceive of such re-creation, in a world sense, except through spiritual renascence and unification of western civilization. In its essence Naziism is a revolt against that civilization — the most radical break in its continuity for centuries. Western civilization is not something finished and static, nor something that has never been fructified by and in turn influenced the Orient. On the contrary, its basic ethos comes from the East, as it has carried to the East both its inventions for good and for evil and its political and economic conceptions — both of capitalism and of socialism.

Yet it holds great promise for the future only if its future rests upon its positive and creative accumulations from the past. It has no future if it comes yawping out of the forests with Viking horns upon its head brandishing a battle-axe and proclaiming as a New Order the brutalism of Teutonic tribesmen of a pre-Christian and pre-civilized era.

Naziism is a primitive outburst of rebellion and revolt growing out of confusions and frustrations, and its victim is western civilization, whether it turns its arms on Russia, where western and oriental civilization meet, or on France or Britain or America. The frustrations which caused it to burst forth are not frustrations imposed upon Germany by the outside. They are *inherent* frustrations which conquest cannot appease. They are frustrations growing out of an inherent conflict in itself never harmonized.

And this conflict has now become a conflict in the East as well; with oriental civilization as well. For again, as Nazi Germany is the Maverick of Europe, so is Japan the Maverick of Asia — the least truly Asiatic of Asiatic nations, as Germany is the least truly European of European nations.

The curse of the West has been the spirit of force, in which so much of its creative energy has been burned. The curse of the East has been its passivity, in which so many of its creative energies have died. Perhaps out of the Axis menace to both civilizations each will find its true soul, ex-pressed in adequate political and social forms.

I believe western civilization to be rooted in Reason and in Christian morality. And I covet for my country, as a leader of the New World, that it become a leader *toward* a New World. I covet for it, not prosperity, but righteous-ness; not a high standard of living, but a high standard of life, not only to be greatly feared in this war, but to be greatly loved in peace.

But I do not covet for it even a *spiritual* imperialism that treats the rest of the world, oriental or western, with contempt. America is far too young, far too provincial, and far too inexperienced and brash to dare claim even spiritual leadership solely. Let us have done with the idea that the world will be led to salvation by the Example of America — to paraphrase the German proverb, *An deutschem Wesen wird die Welt genesen.* The British have not, perhaps, our vitality; they have borne heavy responsibilities too long, and sapped their energies over too great an area. But they have a deeper culture, a longer stable political order, and a wider and more responsible world experience than we. Europe is not an old and therefore finished culture. There has never been a break for nine centuries in the creative power of Europe, in every realm of science, art, and learning. In our own day, and especially in the smaller countries, Europe has made contributions to social democracy, to intelligent domestic administration, to the integration of private and public enterprise, the efficiency of which we have not yet approximated. Our universities would be sterile without European thought; our science be infinitely retarded without European contributions. We must add to our vitality and idealism humility, in recognizing that we are not God's Chosen People, or God's Only Country.

What we have is strength, and the youthful power to be moved by the emotion of an ideal; the youthful spirit to attempt new forms. This, the United States shares with Russia, and could share with Germany were a compatible German mind to become ascendant.

The mission of the Young Peoples is not to put the older peoples upon funeral pyres and perform a war dance around the holocaust. That is a barbaric and impious idea. Youth has energy and idealism; age has tradition and wisdom. Youth is also cruel; age is more tolerant and kind. Youth movements, whether within nations or of nations, are horribly destructive things if they are cut off from the adult world. They jump impetuously into something that seems new, only to find that it was old and has failed centuries ago.

Little of this thinking will come out in these broadcasts, to the enemy who is my friend. Obviously, it was impossible to publish them without an introduction, but now the introduction is consuming the book — and the rest might as well be thrown away.

Yet, what I have written here was in my mind — and growing in my mind — as I spoke these broadcasts in a tongue that I once learned in order to understand a recent enemy, who is now an enemy again. And if I could not formulate to him what I have said here, I have at least tried never, in them, to be false to what I believe.

Thus I dedicate this book, first to all my fellow countrymen who are ready in their minds and hearts to join up with the new 'common people' in the commonalty of Mankind, and resolved that out of this war shall be founded their commonwealth.

And to all Englishmen, Germans, Russians, Poles, Czechs,

Italians, Chinese, Indians, Dutchmen, Japanese, Finns, Jugoslavs, Turks, Armenians — to all men and women everywhere, Jew or Gentile, bond or free, conquering or conquered, soldiers or civilians, who are highly resolved that this world under God shall have a new birth of freedom, and who have faith that intelligence and affection shall yet resolve the problems of men and nations.

And in particular, I dedicate it to the Germans of the Swiss Republic, whose scarlet flag lifts the white cross of Christ, whose order embraces freedom, whose unity offers wide diversity, whose peacefulness encompasses strength, whose preparedness scorns militarism, whose tolerance understands discipline, whose personal enterprise admits socialism, whose democracy is rooted in morality, whose state is the microscopic synthesis of Europe, and who have proved for centuries that the German race is not incorrigible.

PART TWO
CONVERSATIONS WITH HANS

THIS is the strangest talk that I have ever made in my life. I am speaking to thousands of people in order to reach a single one, and I do not dare even to name this single one, because he is in an important position and that Dorothy Thompson is trying to reach him from New York would not help him. But I promised him to get in touch with him in case the worst should happen: in case we, who were such good friends, should find ourselves enemies. And now it has happened, and we have been at war for several weeks. Yet — our old promises, the promises we gave each other just in case this should happen — should we break them now?

Listen, Hans. It is absurd that you and I should now be bitter enemies who must wish each other's death. No matter what happens, I refuse to take leave of my senses, and my intelligence tells me that now as before I have good friends in the land of our enemy, Hitler. I feel confident that my voice will reach you and thus it will reach the ear of a man who is just as horrified by the excesses and wickednesses of the Third Reich as I am and is just as perturbed over the fate of his country and of the whole of mankind. I know

that it is very improbable that you, Hans, should be sitting
before a radio set.   How should you know that at just this
moment I am trying to speak to you?   Some of your friends,
however, will hear me, and it will be noised about — that
regularly, every week, I will be at this microphone in order
to say a few things to a single person.   And so eventually I
believe you will hear my voice — the voice of your un-
changed, devoted, personal friend.

We will continue our conversation where we broke it off
when we saw each other last at the end of 1938.   I leave out
of account our correspondence in between.   You were
abroad then, you could have confidence in me, and so you
spoke right out what you thought.   You were as depressed as
I over what was going on in Germany — over the lack of
any legal rights, over the persecutions of Catholics, and
Jews, and Protestants, and above all over the fact that no
one dared to speak an honest word.   You told me, dear
Hans, that you knew you could speak to me as an honest
man who could give a free opinion.   And you expressed
your belief that I would not betray you and that even some
day I might be able to help you.   And that is why I feel,
Hans, that you will answer me now — not only because of
an old friendship — perhaps in addition, out of cool wisdom.   You know as well as I do that the moment is draw-
ing near when every German will be glad to have a reli-
able friend in the world, who will at least stand up for him
personally. . . .

It is too bad that so many people will have to listen, but
just the same I will speak openly.   You are probably thinking, 'It is quite impossible that Dorothy can speak her mind.'

You are thinking: 'The United States is at war and there is a censorship, of course, and the radio only distributes what the Government prepares. And so what I hear in Germany can only be propaganda and I have had enough propaganda; Goebbels has ruined my taste for it.' But, strange as it may seem, our American radio is still relatively free. Like the press it still belongs to private enterprise and the Government leaves it a considerable leeway. Of course, we cannot air military secrets, either in the newspapers or on the radio, but we speak our convictions and opinions and interpretations in our newspapers and into the microphone; political advice and political criticism are conducted with complete freedom. And so I have asked and been granted the opportunity to speak regularly each week, provided I do not cut across the major policies of the Government and do not betray secrets, and make it clear that I speak as a private person.

Now, that is the way I do speak, but not altogether privately, because what I feel is in the minds of millions of my countrymen. I will say of America that it admires nothing so much as candor and loves nothing more than honesty. And I have promised a great many of my friends to ask a few questions of you and to let them know the answers. Before I ask some of these questions I will give you an example of how confused the world seems from here, even to those of us who have the opportunity and the background to get a degree of clarity. From the German news it is quite clear that an extraordinarily large number of German generals and high officers have recently died, but we are breaking our heads to find the explanation. Our Government and especially the armed forces attach no great importance to this news. They are going on the assumption that the German army is intact, that its leadership is intact, and they are preparing themselves to meet and defeat an even greater German army in time to come, and of course the people are absolutely backing them up on that. But just the same there are three theories about the deaths of these German generals and other officers, and I cannot think of any fourth to add. I do not know which, however, of the three is correct.

First of all, people say — and that seems to be the official explanation in Germany — that the generals have fallen in battle on the eastern front. Here in America it is an old saw that generals never die in battle but usually in bed. And if they are dying in such numbers, the troops on the front must be in a really unhappy position, for I have never heard that troops fare better than generals, or that the rate of mortality is lower.

There is a second theory here — that an open conflict exists between the officers' corps and the Nazi Party, and that generals are being picked off on the front by party leaders who want to get rid of them. I myself believe, with considerable evidence to back it, that the Nazis are really getting along badly with the officers. But it is hard to believe that the Nazis are really so ungrateful or so short-sighted that they will murder their military leaders. The generals did a great deal for Hitler in helping him to get to power and they have won all the victories so far, and without them I should think the collapse would be a lot quicker.

So we shake our heads and investigate a third theory. It

is said that the despair among the German generals is worse than among the people at large because they see more clearly how serious the military position of Germany is and because they see no way out of final defeat, especially since we Americans will come into the fight all in good time with the immense resources of our factories and our science; so people who have reached us from Europe in the last few days explain the deaths of generals as suicides.

I really cannot decide in my own mind whether the unquestioned fact of high mortality of the German generals is due to disaster on the eastern front or to assassinations after the pattern of those of Schleicher and von Bredow in 1934, and General von Fritsch before Warsaw — or by suicide. But you, Hans, must know. So help us, as soon as you find it possible, to understand the truth.

The last time we met, Hans, and drank tea together on that beautiful terrace before the lake, you told me, 'Listen, Dorothy, there will not be a war.' And then you told me that you, as a man with wide connections among industrialists, the German bureaucracy, and also among the officers, knew positively that Schacht[1] had gone to Hitler and warned him that Germany would lose any world war, if only for economic reasons, because the world was very large and Germany and even all Europe relatively very small. You told me that Schacht had asked Hitler what would happen if America should come to the help of England with her great industrial production and man-power.

Do you remember our talk then and how I answered you: 'Hans, we both have seen from the beginning that the Nazi

[1] Hjalmar Schacht, former President of the Reichsbank.

dictatorship is preparing for a huge war step by step. And I do not believe that a few intelligent people will be able to stop it and save the peace.' But I asked you what in your opinion would really happen if war broke out and we should find each other in opposite camps. Then, you said, the fate of Germany would be sealed. Everything would depend on whether the world would be willing to make a difference between Germany as a nation and Hitler's National Socialism. And you asked me whether I believed that it would be possible that in America, even during a war, anybody would think objectively of the German nation. I remember I answered you that there were millions of Americans of German blood among us and that we would never accept a race theory about them. But whether we would make a difference between Hitlerism and the Germans as a nation would, I told you, depend on what you, Hans, and your friends would do, not only on what you would say. I said that one day you would have to demonstrate by deeds, drastic deeds, where you stood, if the salvation of Germany depended on the answer to that question. And I remember that I asked you whether you and your friends would ever have the courage to act.

Do you remember how our conversation ended? You were suddenly very restless, your face changed color, and you said hastily: 'I cannot foresee what the times will bring. I do not know what I and my friends will be able to do. But I promise you that I will do everything humanly possible to prevent the complete collapse and extermination of my people as a nation in the catastrophe that a world war would be, and try to find a reasonable and intelligent way out.' And you made me promise. You said: 'Promise me just one thing, Dorothy: that if the war comes and if America is drawn into it — if this horrible catastrophe overtakes us — you will do everything you can think of to get in touch with me, and I promise you I will do the same thing with my friends.'

We shook hands on that, Hans. I am keeping my promise. We will speak again next week. And we will consider together what possibilities there might be and what each of us might do. So until then, Hans — *auf Wiederhören.*

I RECEIVED your letter, Hans, in which you kept your promise to communicate with me in case our two countries should be at war. In that letter you said that the whole war had been miscalculated. Your clear inference was that it had been miscalculated by the German Fuehrer.

I am bringing evidence today to prove that your statement was correct: that the German Fuehrer has miscalculated this war from the beginning. And I shall cite as a witness the late Foreign Minister of Hungary, Count Czaky, and the Prime Minister, who afterward committed suicide, Count Paul Teleki.

In April, 1940, I was in Hungary. I had previously been in Italy, Turkey, Yugoslavia, and Rumania. I traveled as a journalist and writer, independently and, of course, unofficially. I have never been in the service of any government, including my own.

In Budapest, I had a long talk with the Foreign Minister, Count Czaky, whom I had known from former years. He was terribly distressed about the war, and the apprehension that Germany would force Hungary to become involved in it. He told me that he had had an interview with Hitler shortly before the campaign against Poland, and had expressed to Hitler his hope that no drastic step would be taken which could precipitate an all-European and perhaps a world war.

Hitler replied to him:

My intelligence agents have intercepted the reports which the British General Sir William Edmund Ironside has made to both the Polish and British Governments, following a visit to Poland and a study of the military situation there. From these reports I know that General Ironside is skeptical about the Polish power to resist the huge German war machine, and has made it clear that the geographical position of Britain is such that any substantial direct aid to Poland is out of the question.

Therefore [continued Hitler], I believe that either the Poles will give in, and I shall have accomplished another bloodless victory, or, second, that if they fight they will be rapidly defeated. Then Britain will no longer have occasion to pursue the war, and will give up the fight, leaving me supreme in eastern Europe.

Count Czaky told me that he had remarked to Hitler that the British Government had given its word of honor that a campaign against Poland would mean war with Britain and that Britain was not accustomed to go back on her plighted word. To this Hitler replied:

Why should Britain fight? I have great respect for Britain. I should like to work together with Britain. The British are a shrewd people and not accustomed to fight for the interests of other nations. [And he added:] Do you think I want a war with the British Empire? I consider the British Empire a tower of strength and the greatest force for law and order in the world today. The British pound sterling is more than a

currency. It is the greatest financial stabilizer on earth. Do
you think I want to rock an empire that would let loose all
the hordes of Asia? Germany is not yet able to take over the
rôle that Britain has played historically in the world. The
fruits of a British collapse in the Far East would not fall to
Germany but elsewhere. America is also not capable as yet
of taking on the British rôle. I should consider the collapse of
Britain the gateway to pandemonium. No, my friend, the
British won't fight, and everything will turn out beautifully.

Count Czaky talked to me confidentially, not for quotation. But I feel his death releases me from my word, which
was given to him personally. I have never published this
interview up to now anywhere, not even in my own country.
I tell it to you, Hans, because you should know these facts, if
you don't already. You should know, what you already
apprehend, that your Fuehrer precipitated this war on a
complete miscalculation of Great Britain. To be terse, he
thought the British were *lying* — he thought they were
bluffing — he thought that lies were legitimate instruments
of statesmanship. He also had apparently forgotten that
there is such a thing as popular government in the world,
and that any British leader who went back on his publicly
given word would not have lasted twenty-four hours with
the British people. And in this frivolous and childish lack of
knowledge of British character and British statesmanship,
he precipitated this terrible war that now involves my
country, too. I speak the truth, so help me God.

What Count Czaky told me was also backed up by Count
Paul Teleki, then, in the spring of 1940, Premier of Hungary. Count Teleki spoke in a more veiled way, in the long
conversation I had with him. I know of your admiration

for Count Teleki — one of the most intelligent and incorruptible of the eastern European statesmen. Count Teleki also told me that Hitler had miscalculated the war by refusing to believe that the British meant exactly what they said. And as for the way that Hungary feels about this war, I can only quote you Count Teleki on the subject. He said:

> I am a Transylvanian, and I believe that Transylvania is the most Hungarian part of Hungary. I am willing to compromise with Rumania, but not to relinquish perpetually the main body of Transylvania. Yet I am a scientist and a geographer; I am not interested in tomorrow, but in the flow of history. Eventually we must move toward European federations, and in such federations of free states, border problems can be solved. And I tell you [I quote his words literally] I would rather wait thirty years for a readjustment of the Transylvanian problem than have the whole land handed to us as a gift from the Nazis. *For we shall pay for that gift with the freedom of the whole nation of Hungary, and I should consider that the greatest disaster to happen to my country since the invasion of the Turks. The small countries must bury their differences for the time being in the face of a common danger.*

A few months later this wise and able man shot himself rather than break, under Nazi pressure, the treaty he had recently concluded with Yugoslavia, thereby adding a name to the roll of Hungarian honor.

I tell you this, Hans, as another illustration of the frivolity with which this war was begun by your Fuehrer. Your Central European allies are allies in name only. No common purpose or common hope ties them to Germany; only force — force that must forever be maintained, even in the best case for Germany.

These facts about the outbreak of the war — about the frivolous miscalculations of your Fuehrer — explain all his latter speeches. The guilt for this war is on his head; its blood is on his hands and on the hands of those German leaders who, knowing better, did not have the strength of mind and character to oppose him. He knows that the guilt is on him. Like Pontius Pilate, publicly washing his hands of the blood of a just man, Hitler denies in every speech his responsibility for the war. He insists that even if another man had been Chancellor the war would have been forced upon Germany. *With that he attempts to put the guilt for this war first upon the democratic nations, and failing that upon the head of every living German — even upon the heads of those Germans to whom he repeatedly promised nothing but peace.* I do not hold the masses of the German people responsible for this war. I believe they were as much the victims of this frivolous *Narr* [1] as all the other people on this suffering globe. Their sin is not guilt for the war; their sin is that they did not take the responsibility for the fate of their own nation — that they followed blindly and obediently a leader whom millions in their hearts despised.

Therefore, Hans, I speak to you. I tell you that this primary miscalculation has been followed by nothing but miscalculations — miscalculations about Russia, about Japan, and about the United States. These miscalculations are leading Germany to certain ruin. It is possible that they are leading the whole world to chaos and ruin. That is possible. But the ruin of Germany is a *certainty* unless some leaders arise in Germany in whose honor and absolute integrity the world can put its trust.

[1] Fool.

Next Friday I shall speak about your leader's miscalculations about the United States. These miscalculations have been more gigantic even than the miscalculations about Britain. These miscalculations will be fatal for Germany. You may ask me cynically, 'How much do you care about Germany?' My answer is, 'At the moment very little.' I confess it — very little. Yet I know, with cool detachment, that we shall either all be saved together for a new world of reason, realism, and cooperation, or suffer varying degrees of disaster. I therefore speak to you in the name of our old friendship, and I ask you to listen, and again to communicate with me.

And so, until Friday, at 6.15 P.M., Central European Time — *auf Wiederhören.*

HANS, I do not know whether you heard my last two broadcasts. In them I tried to answer some of your questions. I tried to prove to you that this war was precipitated by Hitler and his frivolous advisers on the basis of fundamental miscalculations. I offered evidence to prove that Hitler in starting this war was absolutely convinced that Britain would not fight and is now deeply disturbed at the forces which he has let loose all over the world. Your Fuehrer has sown the wind and reaped the whirlwind. The present leadership of Germany is absolutely incapable of chaining the forces that have been let loose. All the so-called victories are no victories at all. They profit Germany absolutely nothing. Germany is not winning *Lebensraum* for Europe, she is losing it. She is losing it to her ally, Japan. Hitler is giving away to the Japanese the *Lebensraum* of Europe in the Far East.

Hitler has conquered France, but the riches of French Indo-China have not gone to Germany, but to Japan.

Hitler has conquered Holland, but the riches of the Netherlands Empire have not gone to Germany, but to Japan.

Now the Japanese are at the gates of India. Should the Japanese overcome India, the spoils would not go to Germany, but to the Japanese.

Every weakening of the British Empire so far has been a weakening of Europe, and with Europe of Germany, for the benefit of the Japanese.

Hitler is spilling oceans of German blood to win a great empire, not for Germany or for Europe, but for the Japanese.

Hitler himself knows it and is terribly depressed. He knows that the whole war is a miscalculation.

His miscalculation about America was gigantic. Your people, Hans, have been forced to cough up a lot of money to conduct an immense espionage and propaganda in America. The Fuehrer had a theory about America. Goebbels and others told him that the racial and class tensions here were so strong that America could be paralyzed. The money of German workers and middle-class people has been spent by the bucketful to subsidize anti-Semitic and anti-labor newspapers, to influence corrupt politicians, to organize Negroes against whites and stir up whites against Negroes, and to try to make Americans of German descent disloyal to America. It is fantastic to what length the Goebbels machine went, long, long before the war. They even had astrologers and fortune-tellers on their payroll to make predictions in horoscopes that Hitler was going to win the war in 1940 or 1941.

But the American people are not stupid and all the facts came out, and the result was to infuriate the whole nation, and make it even more bitterly anti-Nazi than it would naturally be. The hypocrisy of your Government was the other infuriating thing. At the same time that Nazi agents were organizing Bunds of German Americans and training them in camps to drill and give the Nazi salute, your radio was telling us that we shouldn't intervene in Europe.

Nevertheless the American people wished to avoid war. Our sympathies from the very beginning were with the victims — with the Poles, Czechs, Norwegians, Dutch, French, Greeks, and British — because we knew none of these peoples or their Governments wanted war or were prepared for it.

Every attempt was made by Nazi propaganda to get us to diminish our aid to Great Britain, but it steadily increased, and always with the support of a Congress that has never been subservient to President Roosevelt, but has often crossed him. Yet so strong is this country's hatred of war that I do not believe Congress would have declared war unless there had been a direct attack on American territory. That attack was supplied by your ally Japan after conversations in Berlin.

Now the Nazi propaganda over here is sneering that our war effort will be too little and too late, and the German papers I have seen from Lisbon are telling you, Hans, that American production is crippled by strikes, and that everything we do will be too little and too late. Every difference of opinion here is played up by Goebbels as though it were a major rift. And I fear that many people in Germany will think they have nothing to fear from America. Hans, I have followed what has been done in other countries and I tell you this — and it is the honest truth: no country on earth ever accomplished as much in four months as this country has in war production. It is something impossible to believe unless you have seen it.

Your propaganda is saying that we have metal and rubber shortages. We do. But does anyone in Germany really think that our difficulties in this regard begin to compare with Germany's? We will find rubber for every conceivable military need. We cannot, of course, keep twenty-five million passenger autos on the roads — one for every five persons in America. We can't manufacture five million new cars per year. But there is enough convertible and unessential rubber to meet military needs. Ford is growing masses of it in Brazil and we have absolutely unlimited supplies of oil and grain with which to make synthetic rubber.

So far as food is concerned there is not yet even any sign of war. Nothing so far is rationed, though there is talk of rationing sugar. My own dinner tonight consists of *Kraft-brühe*, fish in aspic, beefsteak *garniert*, and chocolate cake. Incidentally, Hans, I still have my old cook.

I cannot imagine what your Government dreamt of in declaring war on us. They must know something of American mass production — we invented it. Your own tanks and planes are made by American machine tools. This country invented the airplane, the submarine, the magnetic mine, and Stuka diving — as a test for machinery. And fully a third of all our industrial scientists are working on new inventions of terrific power. Your Government must know that an army of seven to nine million men is now being trained, and if you think it will take years to train them you are wrong. Training for mechanical warfare can be done more swiftly here than anywhere, for every seventeen-year-old boy in the country knows how to run an automobile. We turn out competent pilots faster than anyone. And our boys have a better target

sense than any on earth because almost all of them understand firearms. This is the only country where hunting is a
sport for the people — seven million shooting licenses are
issued every year. I talked this week with an American
military attaché who has seen the armies of all countries, and
he tells me that the American mechanized armies will out-
rank any on earth.

Hans, is it not ironic that these huge armies and machines
should soon be bringing further destruction to German
cities and more deaths to German homes? What in God's
name is your Fuehrer hoping for? Does he perhaps think
that America will collapse? Does he think that Germany
can outlast this titanic nation that is just beginning to move?
Does he not know that normally America produces seventy-
five per cent of all the motors and eighty per cent of all the
steel in the world?

The childish idea that America will break up because of
internal strains simply shows that he knows nothing of
America. This is the most fiercely patriotic country on
earth. Americans say, 'This is God's country.' Americans
selected this country for themselves. They *chose* it. We are a
turbulent and opinionated people, in peacetime. But if
America is ever threatened, there is a herd instinct here
which is terrific. And in this particular war Americans will
fight with two hundred per cent passion, for Americans
have ancestors from the nations Hitler has subjugated.
In declaring war on America, Hitler has reawakened all the
fury of the oppressed European countries. The Hungarians
and Rumanians, for instance, are fighting with you. But the
Americans of Hungarian and Rumanian descent are all on

our side. So are Italians in America. And so are ninety per cent of Americans of German descent, for they loathe a leader who encouraged the Japanese to attack America.

Hans, Hans! Think and act before it is too late. Act for Germany and for Europe and for our common cause. It is not yet too late. Not yet have thousands of American lives been lost in Europe. Not yet has the American hatred of Germany become the hatred of a nation with graves. But the time to save Germany is running out. Your duty is urgent. It is much later than you think.

April 17, 1942

My dear Hans, no Hitlers and no Goebbelses and no race theories and no nationalisms can destroy the fact that all the Germans and Europeans and Americans in the world are children of the same civilization. We are, or pretend to be, Christian peoples. We all have histories based on two thousand years of rule by law. Until the disastrous Nazi revolution, we all read the same books, admired the same works of art, and we all were struggling to achieve a world in which the ordinary human being could live in decency and security.

You have no different ideas in your head or feeling in your breast from those I have in mine. If we were sitting in New York, where the spring is just breaking and the trees bursting into green in the public squares, and if we could talk together, as we could here, with no fear of a Gestapo or a Block watchman — talk together as human beings do when they are free, then we should, I know, find ourselves in agreement, as we always have during all the vicissitudes of the last twenty years in which we have been friends.

There are things that I wish to say to you that are more

fundamental than anything I have said so far. But I want, first, to be sure you are listening. I believe that if you are, I shall have confirmation from you of that fact. I live in that hope.

I am told that what I am doing is quixotic. I am told that no one in Germany will listen to anyone from out-side — that Germany is a world closed and sealed. But I know Germany too well to believe that. I am told that what I am trying to do will do no good, even if it is heard. But I have too much faith in men and women, whatever their nationality, to believe that. Sometime we shall have to live at peace with each other. Sometime. Maybe you and I will not live to see that time. But when it comes, how shall we live in peace if we have not been able in any way to share each other's thoughts?

You told me in your last letter of the death of Robert. He died on the eastern front, you say. You asked whether I remembered him.

How could I forget him? I remember the talk that we all had together in the little restaurant in the Französische Strasse in Berlin, in 1933. Tell me, Hans, is it still called Französische Strasse? Robert had just joined the Nazi Party, and you were remonstrating with him. Robert was so brilliant, and so unstable. He had been a member of the Reichsbanner, then a communist, then a Nazi. He had such great hopes for the Nazis! He believed that the Nazi Party would break up the power of the great corporations, would lead Germany into a simpler and cleaner life, would save the little business man, would give the German worker his just share in the great production of which Germany

was capable in a world of peace and cooperation. I remember how angry he was with me when I said that
Hitler was preparing for war, for conquest, and for nothing
else. He got up and left the restaurant.

I am sorry he is dead, Hans. Never could he have
dreamed that he would be shot to bits in an alien country,
fighting for God knows what cause. Certainly not for the
cause for which he joined the party. He wanted to work in
Germany; he was willing, I remember, to work as a manual
laborer, despite his university degrees, if only by work and
sacrifice he could make Germany pure and beloved of
the world. Remember me to his wife, and embrace his
children for me.

Hans, how many Roberts are going to die this spring?
The thought haunts me. How huge will be the graveyards
of the world before we have peace? And what good will
peace be, if all the Roberts of the world are dead? If
every family is in mourning, and a whole generation
wiped out?

I think of the Russians. God knows I am no communist,
Hans. But never did a country make greater sacrifices in
the attempt to pull itself up by its own bootstraps, by its
own efforts, than Russia did. All the labor they put into
their great industrial plants, denying themselves the
simplest amenities of life to do it: they took it out of their
own hides — not out of anyone else's. Now they are dying
to protect the land that is theirs, built by their toil, created
by their sacrifices. I can understand *their* war. They are
fighting for their own soil. Several years ago I met a Swedish industrialist who was a friend of Goering's. He told

me about a remarkable conversation he had had with
Goering. Goering told him that Germany intended to
take the Ukraine, because Germany needed more land
and soil for its people. My Swedish acquaintance asked
him: 'What will you do with the people already there?
After all, the Ukraine is a thickly populated country.
There are forty or fifty million people living on that soil
already.' Goering said, '*Wir werden sie einfach wegfegen.*'[1] It
was way back in 1935 that Goering said that, when Robert
was still believing that Hitler meant peace. But you, Hans,
you knew about those intentions. But what did you ever
do about them? Do you want to 'sweep fifty million people
away' — back into Asia, or off the face of the earth —
sweep them away as your leaders are sweeping away the
Poles and the South Slavs? What does your conscience
say to you in the dead of the night, Hans? Does it tell you
that no matter what the victory, nothing good can come
of this ghastly thing? What does your Bible tell you, Hans?
Does it warn you against those who try to reap where they
have not sown, and gather where they have not toiled?

You said in your letter, 'No country has the right to
be self-righteous.' Yes, Hans, there as always I agree
with you. Certainly my country has not, Hans. Never in
history did a country have such an opportunity as we had;
an opportunity to be a blessing to the whole world. But
we did not use it; we let it lie fallow; we were too timid
to use our great power. That is true. But we did not
start this war; neither did any of the democracies; every
sort of charge may be made against us, but not this mon-

[1] We will simply sweep them out.

strous charge. Britain and France laid themselves open to
the greatest dangers trying to save peace. But your leader
did not want peace. He wanted power, conquest, the
domination of Europe, the domination of the world. You
can't have those things and have peace too. You know
that, Hans. And you did nothing about it.

Now your leader seems to want peace. He wants peace
with Britain and with us. All the time we are getting reports of feelers being put out in Switzerland and Stockholm.
The latest ones — yesterday — are supposed to come from
a Cologne banker, possibly from the Schroeder Banking
House — from a banker, anyway, who is supposed to be a
friend of von Papen's. And it is the same old story of the
western nations making peace and joining up against
Russia.

Listen, Hans. This is the same proposal that Goering
made in the spring of 1933 to the French Ambassador
François-Poncet: Join us in a war against Russia. France
did not want a war against anybody. It is the same proposal
that was afterward made to the British and that the British
people would have nothing to do with.

The most fantastic expression of it was the Hess affair.
I know a lot about this affair. I heard about it in England
last summer and I heard it correctly. May 10 a year ago,
the anniversary of the unprovoked Nazi attack on Holland,
the Luftwaffe bombed London in a manner never before
suffered by any British city in history. It was a wanton attempt to terrorize London and the whole of England. They
bombed and partially destroyed the three greatest monuments in England, historic monuments which belong to the

whole civilized world: the House of Commons; the British Museum, the world's greatest library; and Westminster Abbey, England's most historic church. They set all London afire. Hundreds of little children perished in explosions or fire. The whole civilized world was horrified.

It was like the *Götterdämmerung*. Then, the same night, Hess dropped out of the skies like Parsifal, with an olive branch in his hand. He came to tell the British that Hitler had changed his mind, wanted peace, and intended instead to attack Russia. And he invited Britain to join this new war on Hitler's side. Hans, I appeal to your common sense. Did you ever in your life hear of anything so insane? It is like trying to convince a woman whom you have brutally raped that you really love her! England was very down that day — but all England laughed. For England is sane and sober like the rest of us.

Now, of course, there were sober reasons why Hess went to England. Hess was the liaison officer between the Nazi Party and the army, and enjoyed the confidence of the army. And the army had told him that Germany should not take on Russia unless she had peace with Britain. The army never underrated Russia. Neither General von Bülow, nor Oscar von Niedermayer, nor General Guderian, who knew most about Russia, believed that Russia could be knocked out with one of Hitler's famous blitzes. They knew it would be a desperate gamble and should not be undertaken with an unprotected rear. So Hitler sent Hess to England to see if he could get peace — and then, when Hess failed, he said Hess had gone crazy. Well, Hess certainly wasn't any more crazy than the person who sent him.

Now, a year after this, we have the same story over again.
Hitler is still trying to get recruits for his holy crusade in
behalf of Christianity! He is trying to scare the world with
a communist menace. Hans, in the first place, both Britain
and the United States have always been able to take care
of their own communists, and incidentally, every once in a
while we find a supposedly communist agitator who turns
out to be a Nazi agent. And it happens that this country
and Britain are both at war with Japan. Unlike Hitler,
who has made enemies of God and the world, we should
never dream of making an enemy of Russia and Japan at
the same time. Hitler's brilliance consisted in driving
Japan into the war and so unifying us completely with
Russia.

How mad it is to send out such peace feelers in this mo-
ment! Look what your leaders have just done in France.
Pétain and Darlan are not sufficient for them. Pétain and
Darlan are collaborationists, but they are still too decent.
Nothing will satisfy Hitler except to have as his French ally
Laval, who is a scoundrel and doublecrosser and a man that
you, Hans, would not shake hands with if you could help it.
Suppose that France and Britain and the United States,
after the last war, when we had the power to do it, had
insisted that one of the leaders of the French Separatist
movement, Matthis or Dorten, should have been made
Chancellor of Germany!

Hitler talks piously of his New Order — and then can
find only traitors and scoundrels on which to base it!
Hans, abandon all wishful thinking. Germany could have
peace tomorrow — she could have a peace that would

leave the whole of Germany intact and inviolate. But the
Nazi régime will never get peace. Never. Neither will
any other régime put up as a façade for the Nazis. Germany
will get peace when people like you, Hans, have the patriot-
ism and courage of your convictions, and arise to help
save Germany and Europe. You could get it now, before
you kill another million young Germans, and before the
whole of western Germany is bombed to shambles. You,
Hans, and all the anti-Nazis in Germany have a choice —
either to follow Hitler into a new and horrible slaughter,
ending in the possible destruction of Germany, or to do
away with this régime and save Germany.

You know that what I say is so. I am anxious for a word
from you. *Auf Wiederhören.*

I ASKED you, German listeners, to spread it abroad that every Friday Dorothy is trying to reach Hans. For I knew if he got wind of such news, he would know who was meant, and would listen. Quite evidently you have helped me, and I thank you from the bottom of my heart. For I have had word from him. The short message that he sent tells me that. And now, Hans, I can speak to you, knowing that you hear. Your message is: 'With or without Hitler, we want peace.'

Hans, I know you want peace. I know the whole German people want peace. I know that the whole German people wanted peace before this war began; I know that no victories have inflamed them to want a further prosecution of the war; I know that they were tricked and lied into this war; and I know they want peace more than they want anything on earth, provided it can be a peace that lets Germany live and offers no barrier to her becoming as prosperous and as economically and socially strong as the great industry and skill of her workers, her scientists, her organizers can make her. Even if there were no evidence

whatever available to us to confirm it, I should know
that the whole German people want peace. I know that
Germany is tired, tired with a terrible sickness and
weariness. I know it because the German people are
only human beings. They are human beings with an immense capacity for sacrifice, and an immense capacity for
discipline. But the German people are only men and
women like the rest of us. They are not supermen; they
have stomachs and hearts and legs and arms.

What they have endured, not only during two and a half
years of war, but during nine years of Hitlerism in preparation for war, baffles the imagination. Not since the slaves
of Egypt have people worked as the masses of the German
workers have done. Yet not even in their little leisure time
have they been able really to relax, really to recuperate
in an atmosphere of freedom. Even their family life has
been organized, and finally destroyed by organization.
Even their pleasures have been organized, and therefore
are no longer pleasures. Every attempt possible has been
made to keep the German workers from thinking. But I
know the German workers, and I know they think. The
taxi-driver who used to stand on the Grosse Stern in Berlin
was a thinking man when he used to carry me every day
to the city. And if he is still alive, he is still using his head
today.

I know something else about the German people. I know
they are a people with troubled consciences. They know
who started this war; they know they have no business in
Norway or Holland or Belgium or Greece or Russia. The
wretched job they have been set to do is not in harmony

with their desires or their consciences. The reunion of all Germans within the Reich *was* in harmony with their desires and their sense of justice. But not the union in the Reich of Dutchmen or Poles or Czechs or Frenchmen. I know that the German boys in all the occupied countries, from the Ukraine to Bordeaux, have only one supreme longing — to go home; to go back to their farms, their apartments, their villages, their cities, and rejoin their wives and children and lovers. I know that German mothers want their sons, German wives their husbands, German children their fathers. And they want sons, and husbands, and fathers with eyes, with faces, with limbs, with laughter.

I know this, out of my knowledge of the German people; I know it with my imagination.

And I know other things to support this. I know that the hospitals in the occupied countries are full of your casualties — of *blind* men, whom Hitler does not dare to let come home. I know that German wounded, terribly wounded, and shell-shocked patients who have gone insane have been put to death in German hospitals, by euthanasia, because the German Government does not dare to let such wrecks of humanity appear in the German streets. I know that your Government, which first tried to discourage interbreeding between German men and so-called 'inferior' races like the Poles, is now systematically driving German men into concubinage with women in the occupied countries and claiming the offspring as Germans, so fearful is it of the decline in the German population.

So, Hans, I know you want peace.

There is other evidence: Your Government is putting out peace feelers all over the place. You personally must know about them, even if the German people do not. Goering is trying to find *somebody* in the United States with whom to negotiate. Well, he will not succeed. We know our old friend Goering, and he is the second to the last person with whom we will negotiate.

Hitler is trying other, more subtle ways. He has sent a gentleman of Jewish origin, an Honorary Aryan, Baron von Oppenheim, who used to play polo with von Papen, to Stockholm, to try to establish contacts there. The former Dutch Prime Minister, de Geer, who was kidnapped in Portugal by the Nazis, is now in Holland and has been ordered to write a book pleading for a negotiated peace. Peace feelers come out of both Ankara and Madrid. Finally, that scoundrel Laval, whom Pétain himself, in an interview with the American journalist, Jay Allen, on January 13, 1941, denounced as a crook, is being used by the Nazis to launch a peace offensive. Chiefly through his son-in-law, Laval has connections in the United States with certain circles in opposition to Roosevelt. Hitler and Laval have hoped to exploit those connections to bring about a negotiated peace. But you, Hans, may know of the resolution adopted by the Republican Party this week, under the leadership of Wendell Willkie. The Republican Party resolution puts the opposition, as well as Roosevelt's own supporters, unitedly behind the President in the prosecution of the war. And, besides, Laval, of all French politicians, is the most despised by the masses of the people in the United States. When this old rascal, who made his first fortune as Minister of Public

Works by grafting off state contracts, and his second **as** Minister of Justice by quashing cases of rich defendants, and his third as Prime Minister by exploiting his office in behalf of his own private law clients — when a man with that record makes eyes at America, everyone here just laughs. We think he could not be trusted with the teaspoons, to say nothing of peace maneuvers. You must have read his speech, Hans! And you must have laughed, as I did, at the way he tried to present himself as a socialist. Like Goering, Goebbels, and the rest of your party rabble, he believes in socializing wealth all right — other people's wealth for his own pocket.

You want peace, Hans; the German people want peace; and Hitler wants peace, believe me. And we want peace. We want peace with the German people — and with you, Hans. With people like you.

Your remark, 'With or without Hitler,' is the proof that you have not really thoroughly thought about peace. For, with us, peace with Hitler is no peace, and we know it will be no peace for the German people, either. We want *real* peace. I want a peace that will assure me that my eleven-year-old son will not be fighting the Nazis when he is the age of his older brother, who is now in the war. We know that nobody has ever had peace with the Nazis, neither the people inside Germany nor the peoples outside. And we are going to finish them, Hans. Believe me. If you don't, we shall. Only, unfortunately, in order to finish with the Nazis we should have to kill a great many more Germans.

Your message, therefore, 'With or without Hitler,' is a

foolish message. Talk about 'Without Hitler.' Then we can talk. Next week, I am going to tell you what 'Without Hitler' means in our mind. Now that I know we are communicating, I can talk about the real issues, for I know that you are at the other end of this wave of ether. Hans, I know you, and I know that you are a serious person. I also know that you are willing to take some risks. If you say, 'Peace without Hitler,' you know there is some possibility. The grandeur of your brief message impresses me. You know, as we all know, that those who release Germany and the world from Hitler have before them the possibility of playing an enormous rôle in coming history. And the thought of you in it, Hans, releases my confidence in Germany and in the human race.

I must stop. My time is up. I will come again next week at the same time. There is so much to say. *Auf Wiederhören.*

HANS, it was with amazement that I listened to Adolf Hitler's speech. I could hardly believe my ears.

I understand now the urgency of the message that you sent me ten days ago. You must have had advance information about much that happened. And I can well understand that you are desperate; desperate, not only about the war situation — though it is truly a desperate one for Germany.

What Hitler in his speech admitted about the winter in Russia, and above all the fact that he announced a new winter campaign — all this means that henceforth he can lie only about minor matters, but that the truth about the war situation is known in Germany today.

Hans, you are desperate about the position of the German army in Russia, but I do not know whether even as well informed a man as you are realizes how strong we have become here in America in the last few months. A friend of mine — a highly talented journalist and an eminent observer — has just returned from Europe. She tells me that there is a lot of talk in Europe about the Russians and the bad situation of the Germans. She was in Portugal, in Spain, and in Switzerland, and spoke with the best-informed people, and she found none who still believed in a German victory. Yet what she reported to me was amazing. For she said that in their pessimistic judgment of the German situation, the Europeans do not yet take us Americans into account. But, Hans, even if the Russians were much weaker than they are, the Nazis would have to lose the war, if only because in the shortest time imaginable we shall have overwhelming superiority of strength.

What I am telling you now is no propaganda. A week ago I did not even know it myself, for to the American people our Government minimizes what we have accomplished in order to spur us on to record accomplishments. But this week I was twice the guest of the American Air Force. I was enormously impressed. We are building the largest air force in the world. I have not the right to disclose details about this either to you or to my fellow countrymen, but our performance in terms of machine power, airplane range, number and training of pilots surpasses anything that even experts have dreamed of up to now. You know, Hans, that the United States reaches from the Atlantic to the Pacific — a distance of six thousand kilometers. The distances to which we are used are larger than any in Europe, and for years our most important cities have been connected by air lines. Thus, America has many thousands of pilots who are better trained in long-distance flying than any other fliers in the world, and now we are taking the best of these and are training them in bombers and pursuit planes. They are able to reach every point of the globe, and it comes natural to them to cross oceans and continents. These airplane crews and the regular army fliers form the nucleus of our air corps, the nucleus of the two million men who will soon make up our air arm.

I don't want to go too deeply into purely military matters — I have other and more important things to say. If this war lasts only a little longer, not a stone will remain on top of another in Germany. Do you not agree, Hans, that it is senseless to reduce all the German towns to so many Lübecks or Rostocks? Just as senseless as the destruction of Rotterdam and Coventry by the German air force.

I am not looking forward with pleasure to that prospect. But I am glad, Hans, that you are desperate about something else even more than you are about the war situation. Defeats have been borne by many nations, and today nearly all of Europe consists of defeated nations. The Serbian General Mihailovitch has suffered the downfall of his country, the Nazis have arrested his family and threaten to shoot his wife and his children — and yet his spirit remains unbroken. For he belongs to the kind of people who cannot be subjugated, because they simply refuse to subjugate themselves.

But what is happening in Germany today? The so-called *Herrenvolk* of Europe has been subjugated, man for man — and that not by the Allies, who have no desire to subjugate any nation, but by Hitler. This happened last Sunday during that Reichstag session which has shaken not only the foundations of the German state, but all the historic foundations of Germany. I am merely citing Hitler's words:

I therefore ask the German Reichstag for an explicit endorsement of my legal right to demand of everyone the discharge of his duties or to cashier anyone from his post or office if I consider that he has failed his duty, regardless of who he may be or what duly acquired rights he may have.

Similarly, I expect the judicial bodies of Germany to understand that the nation does not exist for their sake, but that they exist for its sake ... and ... from now on I will interpose in the legal procedure and demand from the judges to acknowledge as the law whatever I recommend as such.

Hans, I ask you: What punishment or indignity could England or what could America inflict on the German people that could be worse? I am not a German, but now that I have heard this speech I know that I am more German than the German Fuehrer. Here in America we speak of 'natural rights' — of rights that God has given us; and I have found that this conception is untranslatable and that a German cannot understand its meaning. What you in Germany talk about are 'duly acquired rights.' I have always been impressed by this. A man acquires his rights through decades of faithful service, through honesty and reliability, through the performance of his duties, and through courage. Whatever he has acquired by these means, nobody can take away from him. It is stronger than a natural right or a right under common law. It is the mutual acknowledgment of services rendered which connects society with the state.

When the German Empire collapsed, the Socialist ministers of the Republic acknowledged the validity of the pensions of the Imperial civil servants and officers, for these pensions were 'duly acquired rights.' Even the overthrow of the old régime could not deprive a German of his 'duly acquired rights' without disciplinary action. He could not be dismissed from one day to another. He was entitled to a certain leave of absence annually from his work, and so forth.

The sum total of these duly acquired rights has become an unwritten German constitution, irrespective of the form of government of the country. It regulates life itself. And this unwritten constitution had a large number of protectors; namely, the German judges. These judges were not able to prevent Hitler from violating the constitution. They had to pass sentence according to the new Nazi laws. *But they protected the greater German constitution: the rights of the common man, the 'duly acquired rights.'*

Have I understood correctly, Hans? This body of 'duly acquired rights' and of legal protection is so deeply anchored in German life that nobody pays any special attention to it any longer. Everybody carries it in him — and that is Germany. It is so self-evident that maybe no one has ever explained it to Hitler, the foreigner, for every German takes it for granted that every other German knows about it. But Hitler apparently is so unfamiliar with the German tradition that he unceremoniously destroys the foundation of German life, and he is not even conscious of it. Am I right, Hans?

And now he is engaged in overthrowing the German state. Not we, Hans. He.

Do you remember how you gave me German school-books to read from which to learn the German language?

That was long ago. But there is one story that I have not forgotten — the story of the miller of Sans-Souci, whose mill Frederick the Great of Prussia wanted to seize. Every German child knows how the miller answered the King, 'There is still a Supreme Court in Berlin.'

Is there still a Supreme Court, Hans? Can the ordinary citizen still bring action against his King, or his Fuehrer? Is the 'duly acquired right' of the miller to his mill still recognized? Even though an eminent gentleman may regard it as inconvenient?

Why the nonsense about *Herrenvolk*, when the individual among that *Herrenvolk* is subjected to every kind of arbitrary action; when the judge may no longer pronounce judgment in the law, but has to sentence according to party instructions? Hitler now wants to interfere with the individual legal procedures. But Hitler is very busy. He directs the wretched military operations, and one would think that this would be a big enough job for one man. He rules over Germany, and that too is an engrossing occupation. He even rules over all Europe, or so I have been told. Is he going to add to all this the study of individual legal documents and the passing of legal judgments? Whoever has ever had anything to do with courts of law knows how much reading and consulting must be done to obtain a divorce, let alone solve a murder. It is clear that Hitler is unable to do all this. Who, then, is left to decide whose 'duly acquired rights' are to be abrogated? Who is to decide to whom the 'cashiering' is to apply? And what does it mean that someone may be 'removed from wherever he happens to be'? Removed from this world? Shot? Without benefit of the law?

It is clear. The court to decide on this is the Gestapo. And so that is the New Order.

The German man who has staked life and limb for what he thought to be Germany's greatness; the German woman who has fed her family with scanty rations and who now receives into the bargain the notification of her son's death at the front; the German worker who stands at his workbench until he is exhausted — all these have been basely rewarded by the Fuehrer, for the *Herrenvolk* henceforth has no more 'duly acquired rights,' nor any protection by law.

Es ist zum kotzen,[1] Hans! But, some will ask, Why for heaven's sake should Hitler destroy Germany's foundations? There is only one answer to that question. It is because he is afraid of the German people. Long before most Germans did, I had read Hitler's book, *Mein Kampf.* I had recognized that this conceited ass did not understand what Ludendorff knew: namely, that Germany had been defeated militarily in the last war. That is why Hitler accused the German people of responsibility for the defeat. It was the German people who let the military front down. So he thought, and ever since he has suffered from the fixation that Germany will be defeated by the German people. He will not admit that he is a poor edition of Kaiser Wilhelm II who has once more mobilized God and the world against himself. His sublime policy has brought it to pass that hundreds of thousands of American soldiers are stationed in Greenland and Iceland and in the British Isles, that American airplanes fly over and around Europe, and that a German collapse from outside is once again certain.

But no, Germany will not again be defeated by the entire

[1] A rough German phrase that means, 'It's enough to make one throw up.'

world! Hitler's mythology will not allow that. So he is preparing 'another stab-in-the-back' legend! That is Hitler's *idée fixe*. But there are no more ordinary back-stabbers left in Germany: neither Jews, nor pacifists, nor Social Democrats. What is left is the common people, the common man with horse sense that does not allow him to lay down his life for a lost cause, nor, for the sake of a lost cause, to allow his wife and children to go hungry. And this common man says: 'Let us put an end to this! Let us make peace!' This is what Hitler considers a stab in the back.

In order to parry this stab in the back, Hitler stabs his dagger into the hearts of the German people. For this is what he has done. Hans, I am worried about you, for God alone knows how much longer you will be allowed to live. A big offensive is in the offing and many honest Germans will be put to death. So Hitler has had the Reichstag present him with a mandate that will make a legal institution of Saint Bartholomew Nights. Hitler now has a 'duly acquired right' to slaughter Germans.

Will Germany put up with this further humiliation? Will she sacrifice her duly acquired rights and judges to this man? I pray that there will be no more Hitler, but still a Germany, when our boys march into Europe. I should like them to find a man whose hand one can shake and with whom we can speak as man to man.

It is on this, and this alone, that the future depends. I mean: Germany's future. I am not giving up hope. You must immediately write me again. It is late, Hans, later than you think.

Auf Wiederhören.

I SHOULD like to ask again, Hans, what is the matter in Germany, and why is your whole propaganda devoted to repeating over and over again that the Nazi Government is not guilty of this war? I can understand that the Nazis need this material for internal consumption, but what I cannot understand is why it is used abroad.

I heard a German broadcast this week on short wave in which Berlin showed the most intense moral disapprobation of the successful British occupation of Madagascar, and your broadcaster had the unadulterated cheek piously to express righteous indignation at what he called 'this method of making war without declaring it, which has been going on since the attack on the French Fleet.' Does your Propaganda Ministry think we never heard of Czechoslovakia or Norway or Holland or Belgium or Russia? Have our newspapers omitted something? Was there a declaration of war in these cases? And how about the attack on Pearl Harbor, by Hitler's beloved ally Japan? That, my dear Hans, occurred in the middle of peace negotiations in Washington, and preceded any rupture of formal relations.

You know as well as I do why we are fighting this war. Do you think that we fight for *Lebensraum*? Or for empire? Do you know that we have no empire even in the Philippines, but that by act of Congress they would have obtained their complete independence in 1946, had they not been conquered by the Japanese?

And regarding Madagascar, Britain and we have promised not to keep it, but to restore it, restore it to a liberated France. As England has restored Abyssinia to the Negus, Haile Selassie, after British blood was spilt to liberate it. But who in the world believes that a victorious Hitler will ever free anything that he has once taken — Norway, for instance, or Holland, or Belgium? To say nothing of Poland. Hans, your Government is going to lose this war because of its deceitfulness. It is now frantically looking around for a cause for which to fight this war. It cannot fight it on Nazi grounds because the Nazi revolution is the world's greatest flop. So it is now taking up the Rights of Asiatic Peoples — while it continues to preach the theory of Germanic racial superiority. I suppose that it is finding that the Japanese sons of the sun are really Teutons. It is championing the cause of oppressed peoples — and trying to convince Frenchmen that America is oppressing France. We note with pleasure, Hans, that the only slogans that your Nazi propagandists believe to be effective among the peoples of the world are democratic slogans.

What the Goebbels office does not know is that words are useless without deeds. If you have democratic slogans regarding freedom and non-aggression, you must restore freedom and evacuate every inch of soil that you have won

by aggression. Then, people will believe you. You cannot
have *Lebensraum* and freedom for nationalities in the same
breath. We have on our side the faith of the peoples because our slogans and our actions are the same thing. Mr.
Roosevelt never wrote a *Mein Kampf.*

You know, Hans, that the whole of Europe believes in
our promises. The whole of Europe knows that we want
nothing from Europe except the freedom of Europe. I
hope that all Europe also knows that we in America, a vast
and mighty nation as we are, are also not fighting for a
restoration of the pre-war *status quo;* that we do not fear
a strong Europe, nor object to a more closely united
Europe — under one condition, that whatever unity
emerges after this war shall be based on the principle
of equality, and not domination, as is the union of the
American states.

But do people in Germany know it, Hans? Do even you
sufficiently know it? Are these ideas of freedom and equality less attractive to German brains and German hearts
than they are to others? Last week we spoke of the Hitler
speech — of the fact that Hitler had rewarded the people
of Germany for their unconscionable sacrifices by threatening to remove from anyone his duly acquired rights and
his legal protection. In your last letter you asked me for
our peace aims. That is easy to answer, Hans. We can
put a German slogan on our banner: 'Duly acquired rights
and legal protection for every man in Germany, in Europe,
and in the whole world.' That's what we are fighting
for, and fighting for it out of the simplest self-interest.
For America means human rights; that's the whole basis

and justification of its existence. And we know that if
the duly acquired rights and legal protection of Germans
are abolished, and those of Europeans are abolished, they
will eventually be abolished here too. For ours is one
civilization.

How it is one civilization is revealed by the publication of our first casualty lists — the names of the men
who have fallen in the Far East, fighting the aggrandize-
ment of Japan over the whole white and colored world of
Asia. Hans, you may not know that we publish our casualty lists — names, and addresses, and parents. We are
not afraid that our people will quit fighting when they
see what this war is costing. We want to pay tribute to the
men who have died for us, who have died that we and other
peoples may live in a decent and safe world. For us, our
dead are not just a number; they are individuals, who
fought an individual fight; the whole people must know
every name, in order that we may honor them, and remember them.

I have a casualty list before me. And among the casualties are a lot of people who not only died for America,
but who beyond any doubt fought for a better Germany.
Listen to their names and ask me whether you think they
fought out of hatred for the German people or the German
race. Their names are Ehrle, Flechsenhaar, Paul Hollen-
bach, Harry Kaiser, Albert Kurtz, Johann Merkle, Alexander Nadel, Josef Richters, Johann Schuster, Hans
Urban, Edward Werner, Eugene Eberhardt, Wilhelm
Kaupp, Robert Ostermeier, Heinrich Schroeder, Josef
Sperling — and many, many others. German names,

Hans, men of pure German blood, who died to defeat your ally, Japan. And names of every other European people: an enormous number of Italian names; French, Polish, Russian, Czech, Norwegian, Dutch, Hungarian, Rumanian, Serbian among the great mass of Anglo-Saxon names.

Hans, they don't know in Germany what America is. They think this is another Anglo-Saxon people, with some minorities. You must explain to them what America is. America is Mankind. America is that part of Mankind that has broken with every tradition of tyranny. It is the free part of Mankind. It has established the greatest and most powerful nation on earth, and the richest, out of the rejected of Europe, and out of those who have fled from Europe's militarism, and despotisms, and continual wars. Our President Roosevelt is of Dutch origin; the candidate who opposed him and now supports him in the noblest manner, Wendell Willkie, is of pure German origin. And both of them are Americans, first, last, and all the time, and incidentally more Nordic than your whole Nazi kit and caboodle.

When America goes into a war it has a terrible significance, for all Europe re-enters the war. The children of Europe — the free children of Europe — enter the war. And as long as we are fighting, you will never be able to overcome the unrest in Europe because we in America are fighting for our own cousins — yes, and our German cousins, too.

This is not the first time that we have fought our own ancestors and families, for freedom. I, for instance, am of Anglo-Saxon origin, but the American Revolution against

Britain was led and fought by Englishmen, if you are speaking of race; every last one of them men of British blood — Washington, Jefferson, Franklin, Hamilton, Madison. However, we are a people held together by ideas, not by race, and we fight for our ideas, as men; not for our blood, as animals.

I talk of this because it matters in this fratricidal war. It is going to determine who will win it. And we shall win it because we understand human nature; we know what it is people want; all people; because we *are* all people. The Nazis, who never had much instinct, have lost what little they did have, for they are confronted by something that they completely left out of calculation: how people feel. They thought they could make them feel any way they liked, by calculated and so-called scientific propaganda. Well, Hans, you can't. Lincoln said, 'You can fool some of the people all of the time, and all of the people some of the time, but you can never fool all of the people all of the time.' And that's just as true as the great man who said it.

Of course, wars are not won by words or philosophies, except that philosophies give a powerful impetus to weapons. Weapons are growing in our hands at a rate you could not believe possible. Tremble for Germany, Hans! Did anyone in Germany think that there would be no retribution? The retribution is coming, on wings. Enormous wings, and enormous retribution. I know Lübeck and Rostock with their gabled houses. I celebrated the seven-hundredth anniversary of Lübeck, and walked in its squares, and listened to its bells. I know Stuttgart, bedded in the hills, with its lovely villas standing in lawns

and flowers. I have sat on the Hasenberg and gazed at
the mountain line of the Schwäbische Alp, and admired
the terraces on which the houses are built. So much tradition, and form, and beauty — and our great wings have
destroyed it, as your wings destroyed the lovely Temple, in
London, and the House of Commons, and the exquisite
Church of Saint Mary le Bow, and historic Plymouth
from which our own Pilgrim Fathers came — the English
city dearest to American hearts.

Now it is our turn, and this summer, town for town in
Germany will collapse in shambles. Is this government you
have worth it? We have made our decision. Have you made
yours? Will you sacrifice the stones and soil of Germany,
as you have sacrificed duly acquired rights and legal protection? Are you utterly incompetent to free yourselves?
Is there no man in Germany? Only that glassy-eyed
eunuch whom you call your Fuehrer?

In the last war — which you lost, Hans, as you will lose
this one, because of the capacity of your leaders then to
make enemies of God and the world — in the last war, I
say, you could continue to fight to defeat and then begin
over. But if you try that this time, you will not only be
defeated, you will be obliterated. Think of the battleship
Graf Spee! When it foresaw defeat, the Fuehrer ordered it
to scuttle itself. Now he is ordering Germany to scuttle
herself. Are you going to stand by and do it? When
Hitler began this war, he announced pathetically that if
he lost it he would commit suicide. That's all right with
me. But did he answer for you, too, Hans? And for all Germany? For every woman and child? Are you all expected

to commit suicide in the last act of this *Götterdämmerung* that Germany has become?

You have not the choice of a long war ending in victory or a short war ending in giving up. Your real choice is: a long war ending in annihilation, or to end the war with a rising for freedom. It is better to be a live free man, Hans, than it is to be a dead Nazi.

It is hard to talk without a reply, but I am expecting it, Hans.

HANS, imagine my excitement when she came. For she has come, and I have spoken with her. I congratulate you from the bottom of my heart for your energy and intelligence. It was the more exciting in that she did not know that I have been trying for two months to reach you in this manner. In those months she was traveling, across countries and over oceans, finally to sit in my library and say simply, 'I come from Hans.'[1]

First of all, I was immensely happy to learn that your position is safe. I begin to wonder whether any of us have needed to fear the Gestapo quite as much as we have. She even told me about your friends. Congratulations. Now, of course, I asked her why you had not acted. She told me, first, because of anxiety about Germany and the fact that so far there seems no outlook for a reasonable peace, and I saw that you are less informed than I imagined about what is happening in the outside world. You do not know, for instance, the aspirations that are stirring all over the democratic world for a world federation and a

[1] This meeting occurred. All the stated facts in these broadcasts are so.

world government. Not only is this coming from the masses of the people here and elsewhere, but the idea has been launched by the American Vice-President, and the State of North Carolina has passed a resolution calling for the construction of world federation with a sovereign government with limited powers, every country to be, of course, autonomous in its own affairs, and, of course, with Germany having complete equality.

I wish I had time to tell you the story of North Carolina's action. The whole movement started with the people themselves, not with the politicians, and it snowballed up such support from workers, school-teachers, lawyers, professors, farmers — in short, from all the ordinary men of the state — that it passed the lower house unanimously. In the democratic world, where we can still think and speak openly, the people are way ahead of their governments. You must see that the destruction of Germany does not enter into the consideration of any responsible people. Any attempt, should it be tried, to make a punitive peace and not to solve the problems which are at the root of this war — problems of nationality, economics, and the need for a genuine law over nations — will be met, I can assure you, Hans, with revolt from the people of America. Our leaders know this.

So your problem is not the problem of peace — it is the problem of the continuation of this war. I assure you, Hans, the continuation of this war means a much greater destruction of Germany than you seem to imagine capitulation and peace might be. I don't like to repeat now what I have told you before about the destructive power of our combined air forces. It is tremendous, and it holds possibilities that have never been mentioned. Since I spoke last week, two new things have occurred. First, Hitler began what I may call a test for his new spring offensive. I don't prophesy anything except this: hundreds of thousands of Germans will be killed in these weeks. That is the destruction of German man-power and of the future of the German race. For, as you know, your losses up to now are greater than those in the First World War.

Secondly, there is this new threat: We hear that Hitler has begun chemical warfare. Now, Hans, I have been in Russia, and I beseech you: Do not begin chemical warfare against the *Russians*. Did you ever hear of the Ossoaviachim?[1] Of course you have. The Russians have been studying chemical warfare as a defense measure for decades. They would never begin it, because if they started, it would lose them the sympathy of the democratic world. But if Hitler does not take in earnest the warning of Churchill, I tell you there will be sheer bloody hell.

So, in addition to all that I foresaw in the last weeks, new and terrible things dawn for Germany, and for all of us, for that matter. For instance, our common friend who came to me told me of the five million foreigners now working in Germany. She did not draw conclusions from this, but I am sure you have. Have you ever thought it over? You are invaded, Hans, in an invasion arranged for by your genial Fuehrer!

These foreigners — two million war prisoners, and three million impressed men; some of them, of course, those who

---

[1] Ossoaviachim: a private organization, sponsored by the Government, of specially trained corps for defense against chemical and gas warfare.

prefer to eat in Germany where the food is better than in the occupied countries — are hostile to you. No country in the world has such an inimical force in its midst, and these hostile foreigners are taking the places of German workers while the German workers are killed on the front. Hitler began by throwing out all the foreigners, and now he is calling them back in hordes while the German workers are being killed or so crippled that they will never be able to work again.

Your friend tells me that there are many agricultural districts in Germany where only twenty-five per cent of the farm workers are German and seventy-five per cent are foreigners, and that the women, deprived of their men, are turning for comfort to these foreigners and bearing their children. What a status for the German family! The German soldiers, who have had no furlough, sleeping with foreign women all over Europe and their wives at home betraying them. From our viewpoint, we say, 'What a moral disintegration!' But from your Fuehrer's viewpoint, he must be asking, 'What about the Purity of Blood theory!' The senselessness of the Nazi revolution and war aims is revealed every minute. But what can you expect since you are ruled by foreigners anyhow: by Hitler, who is a Czechish cross-breed; by Rosenberg, who is a White Russian; by Bohle, who was born in England; by Darré, who comes from South America; by Hess — well, Hess was born in the British Empire and has gone home.

Hans, when I see what faces Germany, what are you afraid of from us? Have we ever done Germany any harm except when Germany chose to go to war against us? Your friend asked in your name for guarantees. 'What guarantees have we?' she asked. First of all, America is a dominant factor in this war, and you have the guarantee of our previous conduct. Did we feed Germany after the last war or did we not? Did we destroy Germany or did we not? Did we dismember Germany or did we not? Did we lend billions to Germany to rebuild her industries or did we not? Did Germany, with our aid, so recover from the war in twenty years that she thought herself able to challenge the whole world again, or did she not? Now, one thing you can be certain of, Hans. The latter is not going to happen again. This country is resolved that there will be no more wars. We are resolved to build a structure of such equality and justice and so well policed that this cannot happen again. That chance will not be left open to Germany — or to anybody else. This country loathes militarism, parading, uniforms. We are passionate civilians. We do not want to spend years of our lives training for war; we believe the instruments of warfare have become so terrible that no nation must be allowed to use them at its sovereign will. We want our money for education, for housing, for colonization, for development.

Well, do you want to come along in this or don't you? What *do* you want, Hans? Do you want Hitler's dream of a master race and world domination? You will not get it anyhow, but I never in my life knew a German in his right mind who ever wanted anything of the kind.

The question of how Germany can be saved in a peace is easy. The question of how Germany can be saved in war is insoluble.

I made a mistake the other day, and our friend set me right. I spoke of Baron Oppenheim, who has been in Stockholm for peace negotiations. I thought he came from the Schroeder Bank, but your emissary tells me that he is Waldemar von Oppenheim from Oppenheim and Company in Cologne. Of course he is of Jewish origin, but he got himself made an Honorary Aryan by contributing two hundred thousand gold marks to the party fund. This Herr von Oppenheim has been in New York, too. He had a love affair with a Hungarian girl, whom he made so wretched that she killed herself. Maybe that is what got him in as an honorary Nazi. There is great fraternity of that kind. He belongs to the same family as Freiherr von Oppenheim, who was a favorite of the Kaiser. He is a very old man now, but speaks perfect Arabian and is making propaganda among the Arabs, who are Semites like himself. I guess he is trying to make them Honorary Aryans also, or maybe Teutons. If Hitler keeps on, Hans, everybody — the Japs, the Arabians, and the Jewish bankers — will all become Aryans and the only non-Aryans left will be you and me — and Churchill and Roosevelt.

All this sort of peace talk is of course utterly useless. The only way we can get peace is through people like you assuming complete power in Germany. There is no time to carry on very fine negotiations. What you have to do is see the whole situation, realize our attitude, and move yourselves. Because if you do not, there will not be anything left to assume power over; there will be merely carnage and chaos. *Auf Wiederhören.*

Now listen, Hans, here I am again. I want to go back one of these days to the conversation I had with your friend who arrived here in America. But the events have already outstripped the viewpoint that you had when she saw you last. The basic conditions have changed in the meanwhile, and they have changed as I told you they would, here on the air, two months ago. Two months ago I told you the time was short and begged you to save Germany before there was a complete débâcle. And as I said then, it is no personal interest of mine that Germany should be saved. I should like to see our whole civilization saved, however, and that is what I am talking about.

You know, Hans, that I do not regard these broadcasts of mine as a factor in winning the war. First of all, wars are not won by short-wave broadcasts. If they were, we should all have been flat on our backs long ago; because if words would kill, we should have been laid out by the gas attacks of the Goebbels set-up. I honestly am speaking privately to you. Whether anyone else believes it, you will. It is true I have a purpose. It is to establish in the midst of this war that there are reasonable minds everywhere on earth. It is to back up my firm conviction that every German is not a Nazi — and that no intelligent ones are. For I go on the assumption that if there were intelligent Nazis they would have been in your government and would have been able to foresee the dreadful fate that would await Germany if she went to war. I know exactly what the state of your mind is. Half your people are worrying because they are afraid Germany will lose; the other half because they fear Hitler will win. I can bring comfort to those who fear Hitler will win. He will not. Set your minds at rest and relax. Tell our friends in the factories just to relax. The more they relax, the quicker it will be over.

I am interested in getting the war over. '*Das Gute — dieser Satz steht fest; ist stets das Boese das man laesst,*'[1] as you taught me to read in Wilhelm Busch. *Gebt den Krieg auf, und Ihr werdet damit etwas Gutes geschaffen haben.*[2]

I have been telling you the truth for two months. I was amused to read a poem about me in *Kladderadatsch*, picturing me as fulminating in the White House against the British lion. On those rare occasions when I have had the opportunity to visit the White House, I do not waste my breath in saying we must cease to hang on to the tail of the British lion, because we did that in 1776 — rather a long time ago. We are not hanging on to the British tail now, either. We are walking with the British lion claw in claw. You see, we do not believe in keeping up our wars forever. We had our fight, and we have been friends with Britain ever since.

---

[1] 'The Good — so goes the old saw — is the evil that one abandons.'

[2] Abandon the war and you will have created the Good.

Your Propaganda Ministry is trying to remind us of how
we felt in 1775. But set *Kladderadatsch* right for me. I know
Lord Halifax personally and he does not wear a monocle.
The monocle *Kladderadatsch* is worrying about must have
sprung out of the eye of our poor old friend General von
Seekt.[1] I bet it popped out of his eye, right in his grave,
when he saw who was leading Germany.

Yes, I do want war aims, and that is what I am talking
with *you* about, Hans. Not dictated by America, on the
ruins of Britain. We do not want to 'inherit' Britain, or
anything else: not even the Saar or a slice of Germany.
We want a world that makes sense in which intelligent
human beings can live — not one ruled by your raving
Babbitt. I promise you that we will fight on for a reasonable
peace, and that we have as good a chance to win this fight
as we have to win the war — provided we can find a few
allies in Germany itself, who have not got blood all over
their hands.

What concerns me is not governments nor the machina-
tions of international cartels. What concerns me is people —
suffering, misled, miserable people. I know that these
people are the same all over the world and that they
want the same things. They want to live in their own
countries in their own way and have something to say about
the way they are governed. They want to eat three meals
a day, that taste good. They want to have children and
keep those children around them, and be able to tell those
children what they have learned from life. They want to

---

[1] The creator of the modern German Army. He died before Hitler came
to power.

be able to speak without wondering whether the person they are speaking to is a spy. They want to stop having to go to war every twenty years; and if in the world we live in, with its immense possibilities of production and exchange of goods, tremendously augmented by science — if in this world we cannot achieve this, why, let's give it back to the ants. These are my peace aims — and yours.

As for war aims — we want to end the war quickly. How it will end, we know. When it will end, we do not. Goering told that group of German workers on Wednesday that they must *durchhalten 'wie lange immer es auch dauert.' Warum?*[1] You mean you prefer to lose the war with a million more dead, rather than with the present casualty lists? Or do you think the peace will be better for you if we also have a million casualties? You think that will make us softer-hearted, perhaps? Since you cannot turn the tide any more, there is no reason for going on like this, unless perhaps Mr. Goering wants to get a little more time in which to acquire further *objets d'art* in Italy. And even this does not make any sense, because he will have to give them back: give them back to Italy; give them back to the Italian people, to whom they belong. We will even give back to the German people the booty old Goering has stolen from them, and hang back in the German museums, where the German people can see them, the pictures he has stolen from the National Galleries and the Kaiser Friedrich Museum.

But to get back to the war: Look at the situation. That genius Goering said on Thursday that this is the hardest

[1] Hang on, no matter how long it lasts. I ask: Why? And again: Why?

war Germany has ever fought. Yes, and the hardest she has ever lost. I suppose it was just to make it easier that your Fuehrer declared war on the United States in order to aid Japan. Nobody has done that to us for a hundred and fifty years. But what else did the old fatty say? He said: 'The winter campaign in Russia has been terrible. We had to hold the front. And only those who have experienced this know what it costs.' He is wrong. For instance, I never experienced it, but I told you what it would cost. And so did Oscar von Niedermayer and General von Bülow, I guess. But what about the German communiqués in the winter? They were full of lies — as Goering is now confessing. And so why not think they are full of lies now? For instance, the communiqués from Kertch are certainly remarkable. You heard the Russian armies were annihilated there a week ago. If they were, I do not know who you are fighting with. Now we hear you are going to land a hundred thousand parachute troops in the Caucasus. Well, Hans, do you want to bet? You will not. Because your military leaders know that if you do, you will have a hundred thousand casualties. All this nonsense is put out to divert the attention of the German people — and they hope ours — from the losses before Kharkov. What good does Kertch do you when your whole lines are anchored on Kharkov? I do not know whether the Russians will hold Kharkov, but I do know your strategy is in shambles, and that you have already lost the chance of a victory in Russia this summer.

And what was Goering's beautiful argument about why you attacked Russia? He said it was because the Russians were arming, and their mere presence was a threat. Well, Hans, how about the mere presence of the immense un-touched fresh army on the British Isles? This week we landed another huge contingent in northern Ireland. Not a man lost. What do you think they are there for? A sum-mer vacation? I have been telling you about our air force, our pilots, our planes, and their remarkable flying range. Well, was I right? How about the bombing of Tokio — with planes led by Jimmie Doolittle? You know about Jimmie Doolittle? He is a middle-aged gentleman; a civilian flier, with a dozen different world records for speed and long-distance flying. So he took some boys over and blasted Tokio. Listen, Hans, look at the map. Tokio is lots farther from any base we have than Berlin is. And if we can blast Tokio we can blast every corner of the globe. And we have still got Jimmie Doolittle, and a lot more like him.

I based the opinion I expressed to you weeks ago on the bombing of Lübeck and Rostock and Stuttgart. Now I can add Mannheim and Tokio. Must I come back every week and make an alphabetical list? Dresden, Halle, Magdeburg, München, and just to keep the best till the last, Berlin? And all to get rid of your filthy government. My God, does anybody love it that much? I know you do not. But what are you doing about it? I told you two months ago, it was very late. Well, it is later, Hans.

ONCE again, Hans!

Things grow more and more interesting. Last week I had not yet got a full text of Goering's speech. I did get it the next day. Now, it is perfectly obvious to us that the Goering speech not only reveals your serious military and economic crises, but that these crises are mixed up with a political crisis. And if it is not clear in your own mind, I will tell you what it is. It is simply this: You cannot win this war or make peace with the Nazi régime, and you cannot get rid of that régime which you have allowed to fasten itself upon you with a strangle hold. And this régime is capable of governing neither you nor the occupied countries. That is your crisis.

Well, I told you two months ago, Hans, that it was growing very late. I did not know how truly I spoke. For instance, I did not know how bad the food situation is. I know that in the occupied countries it is sheer black starvation. I saw this week a member of the International Red Cross who has just reached here from Paris. She is a member of the international colony; she has access to more food than most workers, but she has scabs all over her legs that refuse to heal. She says that they are eating dog meat in Paris and lucky if they get it; that owing to the lack of any fats, the children are more rickety than they were in Europe at the end of the last war; and that the black starvation flag is flying over the city hall in Brussels. I do not suppose that your people are interested in the sufferings of the people in the countries their armies have conquered, but it has political results. The hatred of Germany is growing daily, and it has economic results. You have killed the geese that laid the eggs. You cannot get any more food out of these plundered countries.

But as for Germany — I see from your papers that the rations have been steadily decreasing, and now, in spite of the fact that you hold the whole of Europe, you are eating exactly what you ate at the end of 1917. So your food situation is equal to your military situation. The Fuehrer has dismissed Darré as he dismissed Brauchitsch. But it will have the same consequences — namely, none. The collapse of the winter campaign was not the fault of Brauchitsch and neither is the food situation the fault of Darré. The Fuehrer always thinks you can solve a problem by cutting off somebody's head. Well, you cannot.

Himmler thinks the same thing. He thinks he can solve the problems of the occupied countries by cutting off the heads of hostages, or even perhaps the head of Heydrich, who has not organized it well enough.

Do you believe, Hans, that a Czech tried to bump off Heydrich? Where were the Czechs when Udet died, or Todt, or General Reichenau? Not that I would blame the Czechs! If I were a Czech, or even as an American, I should be pleased to play the rôle of Charlotte Corday and stick a knife neatly into this *Mordbube* (murder-baby), this international hangman. But Hans, the whole story seems so odd that I have spoken to some experts in criminology — asked them what they think about it. They say first, that the protection of every high Nazi official is so immense that every attempt on his life can only be an inside job. That is true in Germany and even more true in the occupied countries. Second, those who planned the attempt must have known that Heydrich was going to Berlin from Prague, what car he would take, what time he would start, and what road he would take. Well, if the Czechs knew all that, they are pretty bright.

My expert friend said even more: He said that the Beneš Government in London has been continually warning the Czechs against personal outrages, because they are all followed by massacres of the Czech people. If we are to assume it was a Czech, he must have been a maniac or an idiot. Yet, since it was done very intelligently, it was probably not done by a Czech at all.

I cannot decide this — it is only the opinion of an expert on gang warfare — and it does not interest me much; but I should think it would interest you, as it must be increasingly clear to you that your country is in the hands of one of the worst bunches of criminals who have ever oppressed a great people and all that people's neighbors. You are reaching the Robespierre stage of the Terror, and you are reaching it because your leaders are scared.

Now, listen, Hans. Why all these new decrees, unless in preparation for disaster? Your High Command is making

plans for 'all eventualities.' 'All eventualities' does not
mean victory. The Fuehrer is planning for a last stand on
German soil, behind barricades of German corpses. He
is preparing against every attempt to let some intelligence
and wisdom rule inside Germany. So we understand what
Goering meant when he spoke of your 'home front' — the
front 'out there,' he said, meaning Russia — and the front
at home. It is really a *front*. And you are it, Hans, you
and the German people. You are the front against which
Hitler is preparing to defend himself.

He knows what is ahead. Goering says the crops are bad.
They were bad last year, and there is a bad outlook for this
year, too. Nature, says Goering, is treating us in a step-
motherly fashion. Hans, you do not know how truly Goering
spoke. Nature is rising against Nazidom as the forests of
Dunsinane rose against Macbeth. The nature of man is rising in revolt, and the fields themselves. How can you have
crops in Europe if the men of Europe are in prison or starving so they cannot lift a hoe? How can you have crops in
Germany if your workers are ill-fed, and your fields are
tilled by foreigners who loathe you? The crops in America
this year promise to be better than they have ever been in
our entire history — all crops: wheat, corn, oats, hay, cattle,
eggs, fruit, vegetables.

The compulsory labor system performed the same miracle
in the last war. The chickens became anti-German and
refused to produce eggs. Why? Because their owners were
forced to deliver them and not allowed to eat them. In a
free country it is just the opposite. You know I have a farm,
up in the Vermont hills. Well, I am getting one hundred

and sixty eggs a day at present from my two hundred hens, and nobody has asked me to sell or deliver one of them. We could eat every one of them ourselves if we had the stomach capacity. I do deliver them, of course. But my hens are neutral. They are just sticking at being hens, and do not have to give either a Nazi salute or an oath to the American flag. And my farm, Hans, is worked by a German, who came to this country after he was wounded in the last war, and not by a Pole drafted into a labor gang to produce for his enemies, the way your farms are run today.

Instead of suppressing Darré, it would be preferable to give up the whole system of compulsory labor and have free farmers on a free soil. Then you would see a real miracle. You would see that Nature would stop being a stepmother.

But what you see in your own agriculture is true in the factories and in all the occupied countries. All would flourish if you would free them. Then you could buy again butter and eggs from Holland that you cannot dig out of the country with bayonets.

But as it stands now, you face destruction from every side — from the east, where your armies are dying and your matériel being destroyed, from the west, from the skies; from the occupied territories, with hunger breeding disease and wrath; from the home front, where no one any longer trusts anyone else.

Hans, if you and I look back on how this all began, we can see that it began by depriving the German people of one freedom: the freedom freely to vote and freely to choose their leaders. Bit by bit everything has been taken away — every freedom — until at last you are about to be deprived of the freedom to live at all.

While they are all killing each other off, why do you not give them a kick in the pants and join the *Freiheitskrieg* [1] — our war for freedom? Join with us to make a new world! You know exactly what will happen after our victory. You will get back the right to vote and the right to eat your own eggs, and the right to speak as freely as I am speaking at this moment. What are you fighting us for? For the right to die miserably under a heap of ruins? For the right to destroy everything in Europe until you yourselves starve to death?

You will get your freedom back, provided you do not wait too long. But if you are absolutely bent on self-destruction — well, we will eventually help you to destroy yourselves, because we want to get it over. General Arnold, chief of the American Air Force, is in London, you know, and there are great goings-on over here.

I imagine you would rather hear from me than from General Arnold. That is why I keep on talking.

[1] The 'Freedom War' — an old German word.

GOD knows, Hans, I have to say, 'I told you so.' I tried to warn you about the bombing of Cologne and Essen. I could not tell you the place or the day or the hour, could I? As I told you from the beginning, I am not allowed to betray military secrets; otherwise I speak freely. But how far can I go? After all, brother, this is a war. So I can only repeat what I have said time and again: There will not be one stone left on another in Germany unless you get rid of this régime and end this war.

Last week, also, I raised some questions about the assassination of Heydrich. I told you that I did not believe for an instant that a Czech had killed him. It is not clear yet, from your Government's official communiqués, whether he was shot or bombed. Apparently both happened to him. So the assassin was armed with a bomb, a gun, knew where when and how Heydrich was traveling, and managed both to bomb and shoot him. Your Government has even suggested that parachutists might have done it. Sure, that is reasonable; parachutists might have burned the Reichstag, too, if anybody had thought up that argument.

So far as Heydrich is concerned, you have the choice in
logic of two explanations. The first is that the Gestapo is
no longer in control of the occupied countries and is not
able even to protect their chiefs — those Gestapo chiefs
whom they humorously call 'protectors.' The second is that
the assassination of Heydrich was an inside job of the
Gestapo, which *is* in control of everything in the occupied
countries. The first has not happened yet; it will. But the
second is obviously the fact.

My dear Hans, I was not there, but I know what happened, because I know this régime and I have a logical
mind. Maybe my German training helped me to develop
that logical mind.

Your Gestapo boys and many of your generals all know
the game is up. They are now only interested in their personal survival. But they are scared to death of each other.
In that murky and stinking cellar of conspiracy and terror
in which they have been bred, each spies on the other.
Himmler holds a dossier on Heydrich, and Heydrich on
Himmler, and Hess on both of them. And now that they
know that it is all going to break up, they want to begin
destroying evidence.

And, of course, such a breakup is always combined with
new outbreaks of terror. The Nazis confess that they have
not the slightest hint of where the mythical Czech with the
bomb, and the gun, and the map, and the timetable, and
the parachute, and I do not know how many other instruments, may be. And imagine what parachutists! Coming
down with a timetable of Heydrich's route and landing
right by the wayside. If you believe this story, tell your

people, Hans, to give up immediately. The British are master minds!

But while Himmler keeps Heydrich in hiding, living or dead, and probably as dead as a doornail, he uses this *Attentat* to indulge in wholesale murder. And what do the German people think about that, Hans? You write me not to forget that the Germans are a civilized nation. Okay. I remind myself of it every day of my life. Still, I ask you what do *you* think about the wholesale shooting of hostages?

Listen, Hans. Ten days ago was the nineteenth anniversary of the execution of Leo Schlageter by the French. Schlageter is a Nazi hero. What did Schlageter do? He blew up the railroad line between Düsseldorf and Duisburg during the French occupation of Germany after the last war. The Nazis, in honoring Schlageter, aver that sabotage against occupying authorities is the duty of every patriot. Isn't that logical? But did they think that there would not be Schlageters all over Europe? Thousands of Schlageters? But what happened in the Schlageter case? He was caught; he was given a trial; he confessed; he was shot. Did the French or the British or the Americans *ever* drag innocent people from their homes and shoot them because they could not find a culprit?

The shooting of hostages is against all international law. It is murder, pure and simple. In Serbia, your authorities have taken peasants from their fields and hanged them to their own apple trees — because they could not find the persons who had committed sabotage. Whole villages have been bombed and wiped out as reprisals for individual acts.

The same has happened in every country from Norway to Poland to France to Greece. Our correspondents who have just returned from being interned in Germany estimate that four hundred thousand innocent persons have been murdered *since* the Nazis supposedly won this war on the Continent of Europe.

I warned you about the bombing of Cologne. Now I want to warn you again. The American people are *furious* about this shooting of hostages. We will not stand for it. We are no longer in the position where we have no weapons with which to protect the people of the occupied countries. We are no advocates of total war. We do not like war against women and children. Neither we nor any other members of the United Nations ever thought up this kind of war. The world can thank that madman General Ludendorff for the idea of total war. He first coined the phrase and wrote a book describing and advocating what has taken place — way back in the twenties. You yourself gave me the book: it was called *Der Totale Krieg.*[1] Hitler began Ludendorff's war in Poland. Now that the boot is on the other leg, your Nazis are howling about it, about the inhumanity of bombing Lübeck and Cologne. But when I was in Italy, in the spring of 1940, the German Embassy was showing the films of the total war in Poland and the bombing of civilians; showing them and bragging; showing them to prove what terrible things would happen to anybody opposing the Nazi armies. And I saw people, Italians, your allies, walk out of those films green in the face, and in the whole international audience there was not one burst of

[1] The total war.

applause. Now you have got that war back on Germany's doorstep. And anybody in Germany — any taxi-driver or housewife — could have known that it would happen that way. Hitler kidded you along that some sort of divine providence would protect the German people from the result of their own acts. Bombs could fall everywhere in the world, but not on Germany.

Now I am telling you, Hans, and I am again warning you — we shall not desert the peoples of Europe. We call them the Silent People — the people who suffer and endure under the Gestapo — *our* Schlageters and the absolutely innocent who are now being murdered by hundreds. I warn you because I do not *want* innocent Germans murdered. I do not want a German child to die. But if you are unable to stop your Gestapo and the military occupying authorities from ruling by sheer naked terror against defenseless people, we will bring sheer naked terror to defenseless German people *until* you have learned that you can stop it. I tell you that America is outraged, and is crying for action. We have the power, power growing every day.

Hans Thomsen, your former ambassador here, got to Lisbon and, scared that he might not stand in right, rushed to the radio to tell the German people another lie — namely, that America was not prepared, our production was backward, our army small. I tell you, Hans — and I have never lied consciously in my life — that this country is an armed camp; that the entire industry — the greatest industry on earth — is converted to war manufactures, and that the nation is fighting mad.

Back of our effort is a good conscience. We know that

we are fighting for the common people of the world — and we feel that that is what we are on earth for — to defend the common people of the world. If your Fuehrer were not such an ignoramus, he might have read some American history and some American poetry. Those of you, Hans, who were in the early German youth movement, just before the last war — that youth movement so full of sensibility and idealism — will remember when Walt Whitman was your poet as well as ours. Go look up your translations of Whitman and read him again. Read what he said about the American poet. His function, said Whitman, is 'to cheer up slaves and horrify despots.' Whitman is being read again in America as he has not been read for sixty years. Cheer up slaves and horrify despots — that's our aim. And we have both the instruments of cheer and of horror — and you — you, Hans — belong amongst the slaves, too.

We are going to win this war, Hans, but we are not then going to retire as we did last time and let Europe take care of itself. We are not going to come in and then walk out into isolation. We are going to see to it that there is a world fit to live in, as there has not been for the last twenty-five years.

But we would rather make it with you than against you — and make it before the whole of Germany is destroyed.

Auf Wiederhören, Hans. I shall not speak to you again for some time, for I am going up to the farm in the country, and that is three hundred miles away and far from a microphone. But I shall write to you, and my letters to you will be read over the air by a friend of ours whose voice I imagine you will recognize. Her German is better than mine; that is one advantage. And I shall have some important messages for you in these letters. Good luck to you, Hans. Take your chance. And do not be afraid. We know everybody who is for us, and everybody who is against us.

HILDA is speaking. *Grüss' Gott*, Hans. Do you recognize my voice? If you do, give my love to my friends. Here is a letter to you from Dorothy Thompson.

Dear Hans:

I am writing you from the country — from the farm that I have invited you so many times to come and visit. I think it was never so lovely as this year. We are having a remarkable summer — an early spring, weather warm and bright with intermittent rains, and a splendid crop, the best one in years. And this is a very good thing, because we are beginning to believe now that the war will be over soon, and our Department of Agriculture is instructing all of us to grow every bit of food that we can, in order to be able to ship hundreds of thousands of tons of it to Europe, the minute we have peace.

It is hard, up here in the mountains, to see that there is a war at all. We cannot run around in our cars as carelessly as we did a year ago. We have gas for the farm machinery, of course, and plenty for necessary errands, but we shall have to give up the long drives around the countryside to which we are accustomed. However, we have a horse and carriage, and the children find driving Judy much more exciting than a motor-car. I have a number of guests from Europe this summer, some of whose names are known to you. They are very happy, and find that Vermont is extraordinarily like Thüringen, with its wooded mountains and charming villages. I would rather tell you, Hans, about the new calves and the wonderful mass of color of the blooming peonies than about the war and what is going on here, but after all, I must not waste your time.

I have been thinking of the three months, nearly, that have passed since I first spoke to you in answer to your first letter. Then I was optimistic — I know you thought me too optimistic. But as far as we are concerned, I was certainly justified.

Just compare the situation now with then.

Three months ago the blackest spot was the Far East, where we were in a really serious situation. The Japanese were rapidly expanding their power over vast areas, without a single setback. Many people expected the invasion of Australia. That was prevented, first, by the battle of the Coral Sea, which halted this Japanese drive, after the arrival of General MacArthur in Australia had given the greatest possible lift to the morale of that farthest Anglo-Saxon outpost.

Last week we had even better news. For we have won a great defensive battle in the mid-Pacific, at Midway Island. It was, I repeat, a defensive action on our part, but in this sort of defensive battle we have the forecast of coming *offensive* battles against Japan. The most important event in this battle of Midway Island was the revelation that the air arm of the Japanese fleet seems to be definitely crippled. We all recall that the great disasters in the Far East — Pearl Harbor, the sinking of the *Repulse* and the *Prince of Wales*, Singapore and Java — were made possible only by the strength of Japanese air power. So without prophesying that there will be any imminent decision in the Far East — for we do not expect that — we can say that in these three months we have conquered the freedom to act in Europe. And that is a great deal.

For what was in the Nazi and Japanese mind when Pearl Harbor was attacked and Hitler followed it by declaring war on us? Hitler thought that our entire force would be diverted to the Far East, leaving Britain stranded. The Japanese speculation was to give us such a knockout blow in the first blitz that we could not be dangerous to the Japanese for two years, while in the meantime Hitler would have conquered Russia and Britain, after which a two-front attack on the United States would be possible, unless we preferred to capitulate and make a negotiated peace.

What actually happened is the contrary. Indisputably, we went on the defensive in the Far East, and allowed a lot of territory to be lost. But that period is closing; we are holding our own and inflicting heavy losses on the Japanese, knowing that time is definitely on our side.

Our situation would have been very dangerous, however, had the outlook on the other side of the world not improved radically. Pearl Harbor occurred on December 7, exactly the date when the reversal of the Nazi troops before Moscow occurred. We only knew much later what a terrible defeat for you that reversal before Moscow was. It was the complete turning-point in the German war on the eastern front, and has since been acknowledged as such by both Hitler and Goering. It is now the middle of June, and up until now your armies have not been able to start any new major spring offensive. This is very important because in the Nazis' propaganda they have explained the failure of the winter campaign on the ground that they started the spring campaign too late last year. You will recall that they started it last year on the twenty-second of June.

In the last two days there are signs that a larger offensive on the southern Russian front is in being. But there is a difference. It is an offensive with restricted aims. Hitler is trying again to reconquer the lost area before Kharkov, and his armies are attacking besieged Sevastopol. From a military point of view these are only preparations for a major offensive and not the offensive itself. And how much the German army in the east has been weakened is revealed by the fact that it has not even been able to mop up the guerrilla areas that reach from Jugoslavia to Leningrad, with a year in which to do it.

I think there are a number of reasons for Hitler's hesitation in the east. It is due not only to the weakening of the German army, but to the situation in western Europe. Every offensive in the east last spring was undertaken under the protection of a huge air fleet. This was perfectly possible, because in the west Britain was practically helpless. As recently as May of last year the worst bombardment of London occurred, and the British were able to make only weak reprisals. But now Hitler has the choice either to sit with his hands in his pockets, while western Germany is utterly destroyed, or to call back at least part of his air arm from the eastern front. And never, at any time during this entire war, has Hitler demonstrated that he has sufficient air force to employ it on a large scale in two places at once. His whole strategy has been step by step, concentrating everything on a single objective.

He now has to consider two new straws in the wind.

The first is the recent warning by the British through the B.B.C. to all the French coastal areas to evacuate them of civilians, since they are becoming a theater of war. It is up to Hitler to decide in his own mind whether this means the opening of a second front, or whether he can expect a great enlargement of commando raids on many points of the European coast. At any rate, he must protect himself against the use of all his reserves in the east.

The second straw is the immense revival of interest in gliding — particularly in the United States, where the American army is building a great new attack force. The details are secret, but it has been revealed that a large number of glider pilots have been recruited and trained. The Germans used gliders on Crete, but what the Americans and British can eventually do with gliders surpasses anything the Germans have ever dreamed of.

So Hitler has to reckon with the infantry commandos and new winged commandos, which have not so far been seen.

I have always found it possible to measure the state of the Nazi mind by the way the Nazis act. In the whole history of the Nazi régime, whenever they have been on a

spot, they have hit out in all directions in purges and persecutions. It is their way of showing that somebody has got
to be held responsible for mistakes and disasters. When
Hitler was threatened in 1934 with an overturn by the
Reichswehr, he instituted his famous purge. Every pogrom
in Germany occurred at exactly that moment when the
Nazi régime was in difficulty. The persecution of the
religious groups, for instance, has been an almost exact
barometer of the condition of the régime.

Now we are seeing outbreaks of terror everywhere.
Instead of concentrating the whole effort of the Reich on
winning the war, there is a chain of senseless terrorist
acts. What would you think if you heard from England
that Mr. Churchill had arrested the Archbishop of Canter-
bury and had closed the British courts of common law? Or
that Mr. Roosevelt had started a campaign of persecution
against the Catholic Church and arrested leading Republi-
cans? Would you think that meant that our war effort was
going well?

Goering has had to warn your people that the food situation has worsened. I see that rations have been cut fifteen
per cent since April 1, and a census is now being taken of
potato stocks, from which most of the German people live,
because after a bad crop last year, this year's promises to be
a third to a quarter worse, and there are areas where there
are no potatoes at all, requiring a redistribution of stocks.

Whatever can be said of Churchill, no one can say that
he has ever been overoptimistic. Sweat, blood, and tears
was his only promise for two long years. But yesterday Lord
Halifax revealed that Churchill had said that there was a

possibility of victory in 1942, a *probability* in 1943, and a *certainty* in 1944. He also added that Britain had only lost one war and that was to America, and then Texas did not exist. This time, said Lord Halifax, Texas is on the side of the United Nations. Lord Halifax jokes about Texas because that single state is bigger than all Germany. When I talked to you first less than three months ago, would I, or anyone else, have dared speak of the *possibility* of winning this war in 1942, or the *probability* in 1943, or the *certainty* of anything?

Looking at things from here, now, Mr. Churchill does not seem a bit too optimistic. Things are going very well with us. A discussion is beginning as to how we can make a really decent and prosperous world after this war. Almost all intelligent Americans think there has been too much virulent nationalism all around, but everybody is terribly concerned about Germany. What we read makes us think that the whole country must have gone insane. We simply could not believe Himmler's speech about Heydrich — presenting him as a great and noble character who just hated shooting old Czech women and students. According to Himmler, it hurt Heydrich much more than it did the Czechs. Every wound he inflicted on others was a knife in his own heart, according to Himmler. Maybe Himmler is describing his own feelings in arranging for the killing of Heydrich himself. Who knows, in that realm of nightmare that the Third Reich has become? But reading Himmler's speech at Heydrich's funeral, I thought of Goering's last speech in which he referred to the indescribable sufferings of Hitler on the eastern front, who, he said, had to take measures that deeply distressed his tender and noble heart. He had to be cruel, said Goering, only to be kind. Do you know one of the things he ordered? He ordered whole units of German soldiers to be shot for mutiny, because they refused to walk into certain death!

I beg you again, Hans, to use your influence to stop such acts as happened this week, when an entire Czech village was wiped off the map by the Gestapo, every man shot, every woman and child deported, and the village razed and its name blotted from the map. I warn you that there will be reprisals against unprotected German villages if it is impossible for you to stop the Gestapo.

The most important thing for all good Germans to do is to get away from the industrial centers — why should your Government leave women and children around places like Cologne? The British evacuated millions of children from such industrial areas long ago. And, further, good Germans must be very careful to have no connections or dealings with the S.S. or the Gestapo. I happen to know that enormous lists are being prepared of people who will certainly be dealt with when we are victorious. Our great hope is that we shall not catch any innocent people in the net, and you must help us not to.

Now, my friend, I must go back to my garden. I hope that we shall sit together in peace one of these days, and talk as we did in happier times. We have the same enemies, Hans — the Nazis who planned and started this horrible war. Good-bye — I will write next week.

My dear Hans:

I write you again from the country, again regretting that we cannot be sitting down together here to speak quietly with each other.

This week I see by the papers that your Government has seized all stocks and bonds of German industry except those held by the industrialists themselves. Your Government is offering in exchange treasury bonds (*Schatzanweisungen*). That means that everybody who has bought securities of German industry — that is to say *real* values — is forced to exchange them for the worthless paper of a government that cannot possibly survive this war; and that in any case is bankrupt. These shares are held by banks, savings banks, insurance companies, and private owners.

I suppose that your Government is presenting this to you as a form of socialism. But it is a very odd form of socialism, because it does not expropriate the monopolists of German industry, such as the Krupps, the Voglers, the Kirdorffs, the Henckel-Donnersmarcks, but only what is left of the middle class. It is an application of the theory of the *Herrenvolk* inside Germany. The combination of party chieftains and great industrialists who have already looted the stocks of the industries of the whole of Europe are now looting the German people and especially the middle classes, and preparing that the masses of the German people, through their savings-bank deposits and insurance policies, shall pay the cost of this war. They figure that whatever happens as a result of the war, the German industries will remain valuable, and they are seeing to it that these real and permanent values are in the hands of a very small group of people.

The financial policy of the big trusts has been to profiteer from the rearmament by which this war was prepared and to profit since it began by the war production. They never put their profits, however, into the banks, and of course they did not buy treasury bonds. Instead they put their money back into plants, and if they needed money they got credit, of course, *from* the banks. That is to say, from the savings of the German people. They explained to your Government that this was in the national interest because the Government needed extension of production.

Meanwhile, naturally, the small businesses have become more and more restricted because of lack of materials and lack of products, so they have liquidated a part of their stocks for money. This money was then either invested in the banks, or invested in shares of the big and booming industries. Now all these savings, constituting a basis for rebuilding their small industries after the war, have been expropriated, while the big monopolist owners are untouched. So this is National Socialism!

Hans, I crossed the ocean from France in the spring of

1940 with two Americans. One had been the representative
in Berlin of the National City Bank, and one of General
Motors. Both told me that Germany was the monopoly
capitalists' paradise. Measures like this one explain why in
every country the only people who are favorable to the
Nazis in this war, and who are collaborating in the occupied
countries, are the very biggest monopolists.

This measure is theoretically taken to prevent inflation.
But what *is* inflation? I should not have to tell you. You
in Germany know more about it than we do here. It was a
big German industrialist who organized the last inflation.
His name was Hugo Stinnes. He borrowed money from
the banks, and expanded his plants to include a large part
of the wealth of Germany. Then he wiped out his debts
by collaborating with others to make money worthless,
and put the blame on the reparations.

But what Stinnes did was harmless compared with what is
being done now. First, the inflation of 1923 was an *open* inflation. Everyone could see it, and, so far as possible, he
could try to save his money by buying *Sachwerte* (real goods)
or shares. He could see what was happening by the barometer of the stock market. It was, if you will excuse the
word, an 'honest' inflation.

Your Government has now abolished the stock market
and forbids ordinary people to have any access to the
shares of industries. So you have a secret inflation. Your
money is as worthless as in the last inflation, but you do
not know it.

I suppose there are political reasons for this. Your Government wants to have every human being in Germany in

its hands, because it is now terribly afraid of the future. We have seen signs of this for months, ever since Hitler's speech of April 26 doing away with duly acquired rights and intervening in the civil courts, which, incidentally, have jurisdiction over matters of contract.

And it also throws new light on why you are attacking and trying to destroy Russia. The reasons are not only, or primarily, military. They are because, as your Government for once truthfully says, it is afraid of communism. It is afraid of a system that expropriates *all* productive wealth, including that of the monopolists.

So what is your Government doing? It is creating all the hardships and injustices of bolshevism without the justice of socialism.

It is hard for me, Hans, who believe in private property widely and democratically distributed, and in limited powers for the state, to say that I prefer communism to this. But anybody with a head on his shoulders would.

Furthermore, your factories are being filled up with foreign labor whose cheap wages force down the German standard, while German workers are being poured into the holocaust. What a situation for the German worker — being shot and crippled in Russia, his job taken by subject people, lured on by socialist catchwords in Germany while he tries with his life to destroy socialist Russia and democratic America on the side of feudal Japan!

We are also terribly concerned about this, for it will make the problem of German reconstruction, after we have won, infinitely more difficult. In stiff negotiations with Molotoff this week we have reached an agreement with the

Russians that practically avoids the bolshevization of Germany after a United Nations victory.

Roosevelt acknowledges that the German people do not share the guilt of its leadership and *de facto* belong to the suppressed peoples who must be freed and joined to all the rest of us equally after this war. But how difficult it will be to do this, if you allow your Government to destroy all the wealth of the masses of the people now!

The ways open to you in which you can protect what little you still have are very few. You can, of course, attempt to get rid of your worthless treasury bonds, since they are still negotiable, withdraw deposits, and buy whatever *Sachwerte* can be obtained — any real estate that can be purchased, for instance. For the German land will always have value as will objects of art. I do not know what else you can buy, for everything else is rationed — you will know that better than I.

I fear there is very little time, for these possibilities too will be barred very soon.

Whatever your temporary victories may be, the fact is that your economic structure is collapsing, both under the strain of a war against the world and under the manipulations of ruthless war profiteers at home, plus the immense party structure which is a huge further drain on your limited wealth. You are heading straight into breakdown and chaos, and again I repeat: You are an intelligent patriot. Act!

Dear Hans:

I am writing you again from my country place. I am deeply moved by everything I read and hear.

During the past week I have been attentively listening to the German broadcasts. And I feel how fantastic this world is in which all of us live so near to one another, and in which we are yet split into hostile groups by a perverse Fate.

This feeling has grown considerably stronger in me during the past week because of a letter I received from a good German who is an old friend of mine and is at present living as an internee in a Canadian prison camp. He is a cultivated man, a zealous Catholic, and a few weeks ago I sent him a number of books and newspapers to help him fill his idle hours. I am sorry that this man has been interned. But at first the democratic countries were honeycombed with Nazi spies, with Nazi agents who pretended to be refugees from Hitler and whom we had welcomed with deep sympathy and real love, and so we had no recourse but to lock up everyone who might be suspect.

One would imagine that even an anti-Nazi who is at the same time a German patriot would, after years of imprisonment — first in England and then in Canada — regard the British as his enemies and the Nazis as his friends. But when he was imprisoned in England together with Nazis, he was beaten up by his Nazi fellow prisoners and his religious sentiments were constantly offended. The British had to protect him against these German barbarians, and finally they transferred him to a Canadian camp. There it was the same game all over again. Again he was mocked by the Nazis, and so in the end the English took him to a camp where there are only decent Germans — and consequently no Nazis.

From there he has written me about his previous experiences with the Nazis, and this is what he says:

> In spite of all my suffering, and notwithstanding the spiritual anguish that all decent-thinking people must bear, I know that history has a meaning, for there is a God.
>
> When I was confined in that notorious Nazi camp in England, at the time of France's collapse and when England was wide open to a Nazi attack, life seemed to me an ever-present agony. All day the Nazis in the camp made long speeches. But their speeches were nothing but wild, bestial, blasphemous outbursts of triumph and hatred. Those among us who witnessed this with me and who felt the horrors of this war deep in their hearts, dared not talk about it openly, as I did, so that they might not be tortured by the Nazis all around, as I was. But one poor devil, an officer who had been taken prisoner, has shared my path of sorrow, and a few days ago he reminded me how things had been two years ago in England.
>
> 'Do you remember,' he said, 'how these people behaved

when they felt sure of their victory? Just like savages, like
wild animals. It would truly have been terrible if Hitler
had won at that time. And it would have been quite possible. But the Lord did not allow it to happen.'

This, Hans, is a literal quotation from the letter of a
German internee in Canada, a man who loves Germany,
who has faithfully served his fatherland all his life, and who
hopes for Germany's recovery when he prays for Hitler's
defeat. I can imagine what this man must have felt if he
heard what I heard over the Berlin radio the other day.

Berlin announced a drive against the so-called anti-social
elements of the German people. A new purge had started.
But what are these anti-social elements, according to the
view of the Nazi leaders? Not, as one might think, common
criminals, murderers and thieves. On the contrary, these
have often found shelter in the Nazi Party and for this
reason they are under special protection. Anti-social elements, according to the view of your Minister of Interior,
are in the first place the so-called enemies of the state. But
what does that term signify, in its turn?

You and I know that there is no state in Germany. There
is only a party that poses as the state. Consequently, enemies of the state are merely enemies of the party, which is
waging war exclusively for the sake of keeping itself alive
and in power. The Nazis do not even shrink from extermi-
nating vital elements of the German people. To the party
leaders, the German citizen is by no means a value in himself, but rather a beast of burden that in case of necessity can
be replaced if it is killed in the war. Just this week the
French Minister, Laval, offered to send one and a half

million French labor slaves into the German factories in order to enable the Nazis to drive a corresponding number of German workers to a Russian death.

Hans, the extermination of enemies of the state in a country like Germany seems strange to us. First, we know that a large part of the German population is against the Nazi régime. Second, it is clear from a logical point of view that at one time in his life every grown German must have been an enemy of the state. During the past thirty years Germany has been in turn an empire, a republic, and a Nazi dictatorship. The entire Nazi dictatorship was of course created by enemies of the state — namely, by enemies of the Republic. The Republic was created by enemies of the state — namely, by enemies of the monarchy.

We of the western world know that all political and cultural progress is the work of opposition, and that all progress stops when there is no longer an opposition. Hitler tacitly admits that Germany is in the happy position of having an opposition consisting of enemies of the state. The only hope for a better Germany in a livable world rests in the existence of this opposition. You, Hans, are to be congratulated because you have so long and so firmly kept up your spirit of resistance. But your most dangerous hour is at hand, for the slightest attempt to exhort people to reason and to represent the facts truthfully may cost you your freedom, even your life.

I take it for granted that you must have noticed, as I did, that every Nazi victory brings in its wake, not more freedom, but less freedom. The German armies have just taken Tobruk; Goebbels celebrates this as a colossal triumph —

and at the same time a new wave of persecution starts against the enemies of the state, who apparently increase rather than decrease in number with each Nazi victory.

Hans, this is a fact from which you yourself suffer, just as my friend in the prison camp did. Whenever the Nazis smell victory, they grow wild. They trample their enemies under foot, as well as their own fellow citizens. They celebrate their capture of Tobruk by issuing a long decree calling for forced German labor and for new concentration camps.

If it were a question of drunks who are allegedly to be put behind bars, this would be unjust, but one could bear with it. It is not our chief reproach against Herr Robert Ley[1] that he frequently gets drunk. I do not grudge him that pleasure, if only in his drunken bluster he would not continually think up new infamies against the European workers. But when a worker has once drunk a glass too many, and this is used as an excuse to terrorize him, it is no longer a matter of social hygiene or protection of the race. It is simply one of shameful suppression, and I can only hope that his fellow workers will stand behind him.

Hitler should create better working conditions, and then people would not drink so much. But you know the old German proverb: 'He who has worries has liquor too.'

Another anti-social worker is the grumbler, the diehard, as they say. Well, Hans, can one be expected to work seventy hours a week and not even grumble? The Bible says 'Thou shalt not muzzle the ox when he treadeth out the corn.' Unfortunately the Nazis do not read the Bible. This will

[1] Head of the Nazi Labor Front.

have to be atoned for. The Bible, as we know, shows a deep understanding of human nature, and whoever acts contrary to it creates against himself the opposition that will overthrow him in the end.

All those who hope to profit by their long lives' toil, or who want to live off their insurance or have to lay claim to their sickness benefits, have now been proclaimed enemies of the state. This is the first step toward the abolition of the entire insurance system about which I talked to you last week. There is an internal relation between the confiscation of the shares, the devaluation of the insurance, the new inflation in Germany, and this sharp measure against the so-called enemies of the state. No outward victory can delay the internal collapse.

You and I must deeply regret every success of Nazi arms, for though such successes do not change one whit the outcome of the war, they do lengthen the war itself, and increase the misery of the world.

Hans, kiss your children and tell them that these are kisses from Dorothy. Your children should know that I am still your friend and that I will be there whenever you need me. For you will need me, Hans.

Au revoir.

Lieber Hans:

There is an enormous advantage in living for a while deep in the heart of the country, where sowing and harvesting, cultivating and marketing, absorb the primary energies and one knows only so much of the war as the papers and the radio reveal. It encourages one to take a long view.

What we are seeing everywhere is a decline of colonial imperialism. Our worst setbacks are in colonial or semi-colonial areas. This does not astonish any American, as it does not astonish the Russians. Although this country has had its fling at imperialism, in the Philippines and in Central America, the instinct and the trend of the United States have always been against it. Every venture in American imperialism has been fought fanatically by the truest expressers of the American spirit. After the Spanish-American War, at the end of the last century, the greatest patriotic poet of those days, William Vaughn Moody, raised his voice in a great American cry to demand the liberation of the colonies, in a poem called 'Ode in Time of Hesitation'; and against American imperialist trends that spirit has always been victorious after brief relapses.

The same is true of Russia, which has consistently supported all movements for national liberation against colonial imperialism ever since the revolution.

In America the trend has become an established policy under President Roosevelt. For the first time in American history there is a clear determination, expressed in every phase of our policy, to treat the Latin-American Republics as equals, and ourselves, being the strongest, richest, and most numerous of the American republics, as merely the strongest among equals.

The tendency of the British Empire in the last twenty-five years, and especially since the Statute of Westminster, has also been in the same direction. Unlike Hitler, who could not believe that the British would be such fools as ever to relinquish India, on which — or so he thought — the wealth and power of Britain were founded, there have been for years in Britain as strong sentiments in favor of the freedom of India as in India itself. Most of the Indian leaders were British-educated; their conceptions of self-government arose from a study of native British institutions. The evolution of the British Empire into the Commonwealth of free and self-governing states took place slowly, since things in England usually evolve slowly. But the direction was clear. The whole of England with the exception of a few old Tories had become increasingly anti-imperialist, and the British problem has been how to effect an evolution without producing anarchy.

It is difficult for me now to see the line that is being followed, Hans, by your own Government and that of Japan. What is without question a British problem — the revolt against colonial imperialism — is equally a problem of all Europe and, indeed, of western civilization. We hear your Government and that of Italy calling to the subject peoples to rise against the British — but in whose interests? The Dutch Empire has been shattered by the Japanese. But the Japanese are themselves virulent imperialists, who are picking up the outposts of the British and Dutch colonial empires for themselves, and not for a moment for Germany or Italy. The Japanese are hostile to the whole white world. It is a mere accident that they have aligned themselves in this war on the side of the Nazis and Italians. They are taking advantage of a fight inside the white world. We could not back their new yellow imperialism, but Hitler encouraged them. The European Far-Eastern possessions are, as a result, passing into the hands of the Japanese.

From a long view, the turning of the Nazis against China, on the side of Japan, was incredibly shortsighted, as many of your military leaders know. Germany, prior to Hitler, enjoyed enormous prestige in China. We ourselves, after the last war, gave you that prestige, for the victorious allies took away Germany's Far-Eastern possessions, and thus dissipated any fear of Germany in the Far East. The result was that German merchants, without extraterritorial rights, were gradually supplanting British and American merchants all over China.

Just as Germany, had she chosen peace instead of war, and abjured the silly theory of Germanic race superiority and pan-German politics, could have become the leader of all Europe without shedding a drop of blood, and without encountering resistance from either Britain or America, so Germany, had she chosen like Russia to become the sponsor of the liberation of the Far East, could have become the dominant white nation in that hemisphere. Now, however, Germany is busily engaged in creating an aggressive Japanese Empire to supplant the white British Empire, encouraging Japan to behave on the Continent of Asia as Britain never for centuries behaved on the Continent of Europe.

All this cannot possibly end well. For the Nazis are destroying Europe at the same time that they are opening the opportunity for an all-Asiatic revolt. Europe, under the Nazis, is being reduced to impoverished colonial vassalage, just at the moment when a free cooperative and prosperous Europe is essential for the protection of the civilization of which we are all a part. The Nazis have even brought it about that Russia is looked upon by the masses of the people of Europe as the liberator from oppression.

Where the policy of your Government is leading in Europe is nowhere better understood than in the United States. The Civil War in America was an attempt to enforce unity upon all the states of the Union. It was fought to enforce unity and to abolish black slavery. The unity had existed from the foundation of the American Republic. In that there was no parallel to the European situation. The original unity was created by agreement — thirteen separate and sovereign states agreed to create a federation and submit to a common government of limited powers. But in the middle of the last century the agrarian states of the South revolted over economic issues, one of which was slavery.

It was well that the Union was restored and preserved,

yet the Civil War itself was a catastrophe the results of which we feel even to the present day. Immediately following the war and after the death of the great conciliator, Lincoln, a victorious and arrogant North attempted to reduce the Southern States to the status that Hitler is now trying to give the conquered nations of Europe. We even had something strongly resembling your Gauleiters, although we called them 'carpetbaggers.' They were men of the North who went into the South, interfered in Southern politics, exploited Southern industries, forcing down the labor standards and making Southern workers work for less money than Northern, and, on the other hand, bringing the previously exploited Negroes up North, to work again for lower wages than the whites. In other words, we had what Hitler advocates for Europe — an *internal* imperialism.

The result was that *all* workers in America had their standard of living depressed; that some of the finest agricultural land became fallow and eroded and lost to cultivation, while an impoverished white population sank to the level of the Negroes, developed malnutrition, such as pellagra, and became the leading American problem. President Roosevelt's greatest claim to fame in history will perhaps be his energetic attempts to rehabilitate the South, an attempt for which the entire nation has naturally had to pay.

Of all forms of imperialism the most disastrous is that in which one people seeks to oppress and subject neighboring peoples of an equal cultural level. Never has Britain attempted to do that, in her whole imperial history. For the result of that sort of oppression — the oppression now being carried out by your Nazi and army chieftains all over Europe — is *universal* depression. The oppressing nation falls to the level of the oppressed. And this your Government is trying to do at a moment when the whole colonial and Far-Eastern world is in revolt, fanning the flames of that revolt in the most irresponsible manner.

Furthermore, the whole of our white civilization, which is relatively small, is threatened by these Nazi raids upon one part of it. That is why we fight the Nazis, Hans. We fight because we know that a Nazi victory will mean chaos and decline throughout our entire world. From that chaos and decline the only aggressive nation that could win empire is the Japanese, and the only successful national risings would be Asiatic. That is why your wisest military leaders are appalled by the turn the war has taken, and why your most gifted poets and historians have chosen exile.

You may ask why I speak in such large terms. But it is the large terms that will determine the outcome of this war — not victories or setbacks in a semi-colonial territory. If you will think through all the aspects of this war, you will see what I see: that the war which you are fighting is profoundly senseless and that your victory could only lead to chaos and disintegration, in which the German nation would be as much a victim as the others. The only reason why I regard the British setback in North Africa as serious is that I fear that it will greatly prolong the war. The world — our world — will never yield to Hitler. And the indefinite prolongation of the war can only exhaust the vital forces of our white civilization. Every Frenchman, Norwegian, Dutchman, Czech, and Pole that you impoverish, starve, and kill only depletes the resources of our civilization and lays it open to the plunder of much vaster peoples. I again appeal to you, Hans, and to all Germans who have not lost their brains: Overthrow the Hitler imperialism — the last virulent imperialism in the western world — and join with the United Nations to make a peace based on reason and realism.

My dear Hans:

Again I write you trusting to a common friend to convey my words to you by means of the radio. I am longing to hear from you again, and wish to tell you that the former means of communication with me are still open. This week I have had a brief note from one of our mutual friends telling me that as recently as four weeks ago you were alive and active, and telling me further what I already knew, namely, that you have not changed your mind about the eventual outlook of this war.

The air is bristling with comments on the new German offensive. I shall not add to them. I am a woman, neither military strategist nor soldier, and so, my friend, what stands out most vividly for me about this new offensive is the terrible toll it is taking of the lives of young men who all belong to the same civilization and who are shedding their blood for a cause that will surely be lost.

I know that the issues of this war are troubling the people of Germany. I know this without any special inside information, sent to me or to anyone else. I see it from your own newspapers, which are continually trying to explain the war, and wash away the guilt for it from the hands of the Hitler régime.

It is odd that your Government, in the midst of a more or less successful new offensive, should now be raising the question of who is guilty for this war. I cannot recall that this question ever arose in Germany during the last war. The debate was only opened later, after the war, when the question of who should pay for it came up. The Nazi régime has less reason logically to argue about this question because, in the Nazis' philosophy of life, there is no guilt in any act that they consider to be for the glory of Germany. Hitler himself wrote in *Mein Kampf* that he would conquer with the sword *Lebensraum* for his people. Fifteen years before the outbreak of the actual war he announced to the world that he would start it. He said that there is no sense in any alliance unless it be for war; he said that room for the plow would have to be conquered by the sword; he proclaimed that any assault, however unprovoked, upon an inferior people by a superior was justified and in the interest of civilization. And he has always claimed the superiority of the Germanic race to all others.

Therefore, I find it odd and interesting that a régime which prepared for this war, provoked this war, started this war, and previous to its outbreak never deigned to apologize for aggressive war, should suddenly become so concerned to remove the guilt for it from their shoulders. It seems to me that this alone is a proof that Germany is not absolutely Nazified and that the Nazi philosophy is not convincing to the masses of the people who have a conscience, suffer under a feeling of guilt, and are right in asking themselves: Why have we invaded foreign countries? What are we doing in the depths of Russia, a country which in twenty years never provoked us; a country, furthermore, which was the first in the world to repudiate the Treaty of Versailles and make a treaty with Germany? What are we doing — the German people must be asking — in Voronezh, a town few Germans had ever heard of only a short time ago? What are we doing in the North African desert? And above all, what are we doing in Norway, in Holland, and in Belgium, countries which were absolutely neutral, peopled by those who had never in their lives done any German any harm?

That is one reason why your press is raising the war guilt question and frantically trying to prove to the German people that they were surrounded and attacked. But there are other questions. Had Germany been attacked, the common man in the street would certainly have risen to her defense, despite the fact that he might dislike his government. But if nobody in the world ever wanted to destroy Germany — ever, in 1939 or in 1942 — then the ordinary German must know that the only question at issue is that of this devilish régime with its lust for world conquest. But the leadership seeks to convince the people of Germany that the outside world is bent on the destruction of their nation and race and that there is therefore no way out of this war.

Do your people remember the exact circumstances under which this war began? Must they be reminded by us? Do they not recall that in order not to provoke Germany, in order to keep the peace, Daladier and Chamberlain broke the French-Russian pact, permitted the union of

Austria and Germany, collaborated for the return of the Sudetenland, kept aloof from the Spanish Civil War, that was provoked by Germany and Italy, and undertook no interference in German internal affairs?

Hans — during all those childish negotiations you and I knew that war could not be prevented by any of these means. You and I, and thousands of others whose voices were never heeded in the councils of states, knew that the breaking of the French-Russian pact and the handing of Austria and the Sudetenland to Hitler would not prevent war. We knew that it would make war certain; that the Hitler régime would never stop its expanding violence unless such circumstances were maintained that its expansion would fail from the outset.

In one peculiar respect people in every single nation are guilty of this war. The Hitler and Mussolini régimes bear the positive guilt, but there is a negative guilt as well. Everyone is guilty for this war who has collaborated for an instant with a régime whose purpose from the beginning was to wage war upon the whole human race. All those who tolerated the disgusting attacks upon the German Jews; all those who stood by and saw the lovers and apostles of peace put in concentration camps, persecuted, and exiled, and uttered no word of protest; all those who stood by and saw the law suspended in Germany, saw the Christian faith flouted and scorned, saw pastors and priests accused, saw fake fires started as an excuse for new outbreaks of terror — saw all this and averted their eyes — all are guilty for the terrible destruction that has overtaken our common world.

All those are guilty who sought to save their own skins at

the expense of others; who denounced their friends, hoping to curry favor with the authorities; who smiled upon the Hitler régime because they saw in it a powerful instrument for suppressing the hard-won rights of working men; all who, admiring the outward panoply of seeming strength, denied with their tongues what they believed in their inmost hearts — all are guilty for this terrible destiny that is obliterating the white race.

Yet many who shared this guilt have exculpated it. Too late to save the peace, they have gone to the aid of the attacked; too late to have saved the peace in a common front, they have organized themselves for a common resistance. They have not thereby escaped the punishment of their guilt; they have paid and are paying in blood. But they have redeemed their own honor and the honor of their nations. But who in Germany will redeem his own honor and that of Germany? Who in Germany is raising his voice against the blood baths in Czechoslovakia and Poland and throughout Europe?

It is as true now as it was before the war began that there are only two ways to peace: a peace *against* Germany or a peace *with* Germany. It must be obvious to you that there can be no peace for Germany and her satellite Italy *against* all of Europe, and all of the English-speaking world.

And it must be clear to you, Hans, that there can be no peace *with* Germany except with such a Germany as is compatible with peace.

This war occurred because of an attempt of the outside world to make peace with a German régime with whom it is impossible to have peace, either externally or internally.

One would think that as the war progresses it would at least be possible for the German people to make peace with the Hitler régime. Yet this régime continues war against the German people themselves, suppressing even the mildest criticism and opposition. It cannot make peace with the peoples it has conquered, but incites and provokes them to continued resistance.

War guilt is not *one* act because of which a people is damned. It can diminish or increase according to the day-to-day behavior. The first German troops that marched into Prague, in violation of a solemn pledge openly given by Hitler, in his own voice, to the whole world, performed a guilty act. The first German troops that crossed the Polish frontier set off this war. But to those first guilty acts, others have been added in geometrical progression. The total incapacity of your lawless régime to create law and order anywhere has led it to acts of unparalleled terror. And every nation that has suffered an unprovoked attack brings in its own separate bill, its own separate charge of guilt against Germany. Your own soldiers have died in Norway, asking their attending priests or physicians in their last gasp for a statement of the truth: 'Is it true,' they have whispered, 'that the British were here first, and we only came to drive them out?' And when the answer was given: '*No*. The British did not invade Norway'; your soldiers, Hans, died with tears on their cheeks and the guilt of their nation in their eyes.

The guilt is rolling up like a vast dirty brown wave. It is engulfing your whole people. Is there in all history a guilt like that committed against the village of Lidice, which was razed to the ground, where every male was murdered and every woman and child deported? And all because a wretched terrorist, Reinhard Heydrich, was shot? And shot by whom? Do you know? Does anybody know? Your régime announced it had apprehended the culprits. But did it publish their names? And afterward, it committed this crime that, like the offense of the King in *Hamlet*, stinks to high heaven.

Do you associate yourself with this guilt, Hans? Do the German people who may hear me associate themselves with that guilt? And if not, how do you dissociate yourselves? Do you go on saying 'Heil Hitler'? If you do, you accept the guilt.

In your last communication you asked me to investigate every way leading to peace. I tell you the only way that will lead to peace. Repudiate this régime, and ask for a peace of equality. Ask for it now before millions more are dead. Ask for it before new cities are destroyed. Ask for it before the whole of our civilization smoulders in ruins. Ask for it before the hatred and will to revenge grow out of all bounds. Ask for it before a war so lightly and arrogantly started by your Fuehrer has bled our whole race white; before the men and women of western civilization, once the world's pride, live in caves to escape attacks from the air, lose every human expression from their faces, and settle into sullen torpor, knowing no art but the art of killing, no science but the science of destruction, no religion but the religion of revenge, no hope but the desperate hope of mere survival.

My dear Hans:

By chance I received this week a letter from a friend in Moscow — a journalist who wrote most objectively. What interested me was not what he said about the military situation, about which, as a matter of fact, he knew no more than we do here, but what he wrote about the changes taking place in Russia, and the mental attitude of the people. And his words were only another proof of the outstanding fact of this war — the fantastic miscalculations of your Fuehrer about the psychology of other nations.

We spoke a long time ago about his miscalculations regarding England — about his opinion, testified to by the late Counts Csaki and Teleki, that England would not really pursue the war; that England would not fight over Poland. Just as great have been his miscalculations about Russia. I do not speak of his serious miscalculations regarding the state of the Russian armaments. I refer to his total misunderstanding of the Russian Revolution.

This misunderstanding arose from two *idées fixes*: the first — expressed in *Mein Kampf* — that Russia was run by Jews and as a result was ripe for ruin; and the second, the belief that the Slavs have no capacities to build a state and that Russia can be ruled only by Germans. The first was nonsense; the second indicated no understanding whatever of Russian history during the last three hundred years.

Actually the Russian Revolution released the Russian national spirit in a terrific manner. My friend writes me that the war has brought about a tremendous renaissance of national pride and that the youth of the nation, for years accustomed to think of Russian history as beginning with the October, 1917, Revolution, are delving into the pre-revolutionary past, and rediscovering all the Russian national heroes. This is a startling contrast to the attitude of the twenties and thirties that regarded the leading characters of the past as nothing but social parasites with no claim to the respect of the New Russia. Alexei Tolstoy, he says, has just finished a play in which he describes Ivan the First as representative of the Russian spirit in all its grandiosity of fervid will and inexhaustible possibilities and powers.

Of course every objective and critical mind that has visited Russia in the last years realized that the Russian Revolution had released in Russia a new vitality and will, a passionate interest in education and exploration, and a faith in a great future, all indicating that Russia was coming into her own as one of the great nations of the earth. Your writer, Prince Rohan, realized this way back in the twenties. So did your first ambassador to the Soviet Union, Count Brockdorf-Rantzau, with whom I had many an interesting talk on this subject. Count Brockdorf-Rantzau believed that the Russian Government was the most incorruptible on earth, and he worked indefatigably that Germany should never make the terrible mistake of putting Russia in the camp of her enemies. He must be turning over in his grave at the policy which has been pursued by the ignoramuses that govern Germany.

In the end, Hans, the outcome of this war will be determined by many factors other than the purely military. If there is any country on earth that *ought* to realize this, it is Germany. Great and vital nations cannot be permanently defeated. Disaster only reawakens in them a passionate will for rebirth.

And among the nations that cannot be defeated two are pre-eminent: Russia and the United States. For both are continental nations, of immense size and immense vitality and youth. And the effect of the war is merely to purge such countries of any weaknesses that might have grown up in peace and weld them into bodies with but a single will.

The history of Russia over the last three hundred years — three hundred years in which there has been many a temporary setback and defeat — is the story of a steady and phenomenal rise. It captured the attention and admiration of an American military genius who wrote at the end of the last century, Homer Lea. Oddly enough, Homer Lea has often been quoted by the Nazis. He pointed out that in the nineteenth century, to gain control over the Caucasus and the Caspian, Russia fought two wars with Persia and a war of sixty-two years with the Highlanders of the Caucasus. This Caucasus, which took sixty-two years to subdue, Hitler hopes to obtain by a blitzkrieg of a few weeks. In the nineteenth century, Russia lost two million out of five million troops engaged in her wars. Yet the Russian population, which at the beginning of the eighteenth century was only twelve million, is today nearly two hundred million.

It is fantastic that Hitler, who realized that defeat for the Germans would only mean a fanatical rebirth of the nationalist spirit, should think that defeat for other nations would mean decadence and decay. There are nations whose time in history passes; they disappear. But Russia is not such a nation. Her time in history, and the time of all the Slavic peoples, is dawning; your best minds and your scholars know this — hence their distress about the war.

Russia does not end at the Urals. It ends at the Pacific. Never will you be able to destroy the Russian armies.

Hitler is without any political ideas regarding the territory he hopes to conquer. In Berlin he has been playing with white Russians, broken-down aristocrats — the very people who have already failed in history. He gets his advice from another embittered White Russian, Alfred Rosenberg. He dreams of setting up a Ukrainian state under German suzerainty, with some subservient hetman as its leader, on the style of the Quisling régime in Norway.

Good God! Even in the last war, when Germany held the Ukraine and the Caucasus and everything for which you are now fighting, this did not work. And the last war brought about the collapse of a rotten and outlived Russian régime. How ridiculous to think that it will work now, even should the Russian armies be pushed back! In the meanwhile a national saga has been born; the Russian has discovered once and for all that he is a Russian — a Great Russian — not a particularist. The soil of the Ukraine is fertilized by heroic Russian blood, out of which will spring the seeds of continual rebellion.

Even now it takes thousands and thousands of German troops to keep Yugoslavia in hand. How many do you think it would take to keep Russia in hand?

The Gestapo is at its wits' end already as to how to govern the conquered nations. It has no instrument but terror, and, again, the German experience itself ought to reveal to you that terror is the most hopeless of instruments against an awakening nation. Every terrorist act becomes a national myth and an instrument for awakening the nation. Thus, every hostage shot in France contributes to the revival of French nationalism and resistance; the same is true of Czechoslovakia. The razing of Lidice, the killing of every man, the imprisoning of every woman, and the throwing of every child into a reform school has simply given the Czech national spirit a rallying cry.

Carlyle, the British writer and historian whom the Nazis profess to admire, and who was certainly greatly admired by Houston Stewart Chamberlain, once said, 'There is no passion of the mind of man but meets and masters the fear of death.' That is so. But the net effect of your war is to raise the national passions of every conquered people to a white heat of will and resolution. The result is that the more you conquer, the greater the eventual retribution for Germany. The result of your victory would only be that eighty million Germans would live in an ocean of four hundred million surrounding enemies, that no individual German in any occupied country would ever be safe; that weapons would grow in the hands of the conquered; that the open war would degenerate into a continual underground revolt, and that the whole of Europe would degenerate into a chaos, without any legal, political, or economic order.

I know that this vision haunts your dreams, as it haunts the dreams of every thoughtful German. The Nazi revolution has failed. In his lucid moments, Hitler knows this himself. He actually expected to be received in Paris and in Oslo, in Moscow and in The Hague, with flowers in his path. He expected everywhere a Nazi revolution. What nonsense! Can he not see that the only dynamic idea in the whole of National Socialism is *nationalism?* Can he not see that even Nazi revolutions in Europe would therefore turn against the suppressors of the nations?

Hitler believed and said that the modern world could only be conquered by the force of a new and dynamic idea. But the dynamic idea in today's world is Freedom — national freedom and personal freedom. Perhaps he hoped to unite Europe. He has done so. He has united it against him — and the world against him.

I find the outlook very dark — very dark for all of us, but darkest of all for Germany. Your military gains of the week do not in the least impress me nor change my opinion, as I am sure they have not changed yours. Your régime is fighting history; it is fighting the deepest instincts of mankind. Every new government you set up in conquered territory is manned by increasingly inferior figureheads, representing the deepest reaction and cynicism. The New Order would therefore be an order of mediocre satraps and sadists ruling by terror. In such a world a victorious German people hope to live — after they have defeated Russia, China, Great Britain, and the United States of America.

Only a revolution for freedom in Germany can prevent German extinction in one way or in another and save Europe and the world from further bloodshed and further chaos. You know this as well as I. What some of your writers have praised in the Nazis as the 'driving power of the will' is proving to be a driving power of the will to death and chaos — the will to extinction in a burning and devastated world.

We were so near to the birth of a new age of freedom and cooperative international rebuilding! Now what do you see ahead, my friend?

I still see that new age ahead, after all the travail. But it presupposes one of two things: our victory, after however prolonged and terrible a struggle — or a German revolution.

So it seems to me, writing and thinking in the calmness of this peaceful countryside, surrounded by men and women who can still think calmly and objectively.

Auf Wiederhören. You have my affection and faith, as always.

My dear Hans:

You ask for news — for facts. Very well, I will bring you some news with comment from the Nazi front in the United States. Did you know that you had opened a front here? I don't mean you, of course, or the German people, but the international Fascist Nazi conspiracy that started this war.

We have been invaded, Hans. It was by only a very small force — a few men. They landed from submarines. Then they established contact with the Fifth Column that had already been organized here, taking advantage of the tolerance and good will of the American people. It was a piece of good luck that they did this, because strange as it may seem our authorities had already become suspicious of certain people. It is not our habit to arrest people upon suspicion, however, but tolerant as we are we certainly do arrest them when they are acting as the agents of invaders.

Two of them were captured by a twenty-one-year-old boy who thought it strange that men should be walking out

of the sea in bathing-suits at dawn and making signs to
others on the shore. It was very funny. Confronted by an
innocent question as to what they were doing there, they
first gave an ambiguous answer. Then the boy asked another innocent question — Had they been clamming? That
gave them the answer, so they said Yes. The boy, however, knew that never a clam had been found in those
waters. They saw his doubt and then threatened to kill
him. He suggested that that would create suspicion.
Then they offered him three hundred dollars to keep his
mouth shut. So he took the three hundred and went to
the police. The police caught the invaders and he found
they had cheated him and given him only two hundred
and sixty dollars. Typical Nazi story.

The lot of them, landing on different parts of the coast,
had been sent over to give instructions to the Fifth Column organized here years ago.

Hans, it must seem odd to you that this Fifth Column
has so far not accomplished a single major objective. So
our free country must be better organized than totalitarian
minds can understand. And maybe Americans are not so
hopelessly stupid. Or do your people really think that the
only way to keep order is to throw into prison or concentration camp anyone who is merely denounced by one of
his neighbors?

However, let's look at what has happened, for it must
interest you. I see that the controlled Nazi press is making
an enormous effort to prove that they, the Nazis, are not
responsible for the war, and that the war is a plot of the
democracies. Now you, Hans, are a logical man, and this

little invasion and what it has revealed prove to you and
to all intelligent men that this war has been plotted for
years by an international Nazi conspiracy.

With whom did these invaders get in touch in the United
States? With American citizens. And who were these
American citizens? They were original members of the
Nazi Party in Germany, who came to this country back in
the twenties as agents of a private Nazi Gestapo which was
working all over the world before it had even succeeded
in imposing its will on Germany.

These party agents were ordered to deflect suspicion
from themselves by becoming American citizens. What
do you have to do to become an American citizen? You
have to swear allegiance to the democratic principles
of this country and swear to defend it in war. So these
people, posing as sincere democrats, obtained the protection of the United States Government, in order to betray
this nation.

They came here — almost all of them — in the twenties.
At that time the United States and Germany were on the
best possible footing. War was the last thing in anybody's
mind — in our mind, or in the mind of the German people.
We had made immense loans to Germany, and America
was taking the lead in bringing about the abolition of
reparations and the reduction of armaments and establishing a peaceful and orderly world. Yet the Nazi Party was
already planting spies and saboteurs in the United States
with orders to await the moment when they would go into
action.

Now I ask you — why? The Nazis intended to come to

power in Germany in order to make war. They were preparing for that war before they were even in power in
Germany. And this little incident establishes the war guilt
of the Nazi Party beyond question of a doubt. Were we
planting saboteurs in Germany in the twenties? Or the
early thirties? Have you ever caught any Englishmen posing as Germans and found they were sent there by Mr.
Churchill or somebody else, in the middle of peace, to prepare to blow up factories when war came? Have you ever
caught any Americans? There were many Czechs and
Poles naturalized in Germany in the twenties. Did you
ever find that they were members of an organization planning to blow up German factories when war came?

How do you think Americans feel when this becomes revealed? It was not necessary to prove to America that the
Nazis are guilty of this war, but it was necessary to demonstrate the methods, the intrigues, the plots, by which the
Nazis prepared this war, for Americans find it very difficult
to believe this kind of thing, having built a civilization and
a great country on mutual trust. This is a country where
there is no such thing as a *carte d'identité*. People have no
papers, unless they want to travel abroad where papers are
required. Even in time of war, classes are not called up
from an already existing police registration. It is merely
announced in the papers that they are wanted and that
they should present themselves; and they come, millions of
them, and there is almost no draft evasion.

It is easy to plant in such a society a spy and sabotage
system, for we are accustomed to taking people on their
own word, on their own oath, believing in the honor of

mankind. So, as I say, it is easy to plant a Fifth Column in such a society. It is not so easy to understand why it does not work, why we caught the invaders and their contacts, and you with your huge Gestapo of three quarters of a million men cannot catch the men who killed Heydrich, must throw people wholesale into concentration camps on the merest suspicion, and resort to shooting innocent hostages.

The answer, my dear Hans, lies in the nature of man. Your system creates bad will and universal suspicion. And in universal suspicion you cannot catch the real culprits at all. There is probably in all Germany not a single living soul who is not guilty of *some* transgression against the Nazi rule. Practically everyone has bought on the black market. Millions have listened to foreign broadcasts. Millions, God bless them, have kept to themselves information that would injure their neighbors. Hundreds of thousands, God bless them, have protected persecuted and hounded Jews. Millions have grumbled at this regulation or that. And so you have a nation that is universally guilty of breaking some decree or other, and all the Nazis can think of doing is to increase the number of the decrees and the penalties and so increase the number of the guilty and give them increased reasons for being more circumspect. After having filled all the concentration camps and all the prisons, the latest measure, I read, is to send malcontents to the Russian front.

In America you can do almost everything — criticize Roosevelt, criticize the war aims, criticize the conduct of the war, criticize the rationing system, ask for new leadership, and even say a good word for the Germans. And the result is that if you are really a traitor everybody knows it, and everybody tells; for the language of criticism differs from the language of treason.

The second result is that everyone has something to defend. He has to defend this world where he is a free man. He has to defend a world where he can live and trust his neighbors because that is the only way a civilized man can live.

So the Nazi invasion makes clear to everybody — to the simplest man — what our aims in this war are. It is to create a society where you do not have to fear that the electrician who comes in to fix your telephone has really come to install a dictaphone, or the porter who is presumably there to answer the door is not really there to read your mail. It is to live again in free air instead of in a conspiracy where no one can trust anyone else.

That leads me to what you and I have known from the beginning. You and I are not enemies. We have a common foe. It is the same foe that got you into this war and got me into this war; and in exactly the same way. That foe, the International Fascists, sent spies among you; undermined your institutions; plotted your war; and sent spies among us; tried to undermine our institutions and prepare us to be the victims of this war.

The victory of this common foe cannot be your victory. It would be your defeat as much as our defeat. For it would be the defeat of what was once our common world — the world of mutual trust and brotherhood.

The war would be finished if the German people would understand this one thing: that they are not fighting for their victory; they are fighting for their defeat. They are not fighting to end war, but to make it perpetual. They are not fighting to win freedom, but to lose it forever. They are fighting for the protection of the Nazi Party and the Gestapo, which can only succeed in oppressing you if it can oppress all the rest of us, too.

Hans — I know you. You would emigrate from Germany after a Nazi victory. Millions of German workers would emigrate from a victorious Germany after a Nazi victory, if there were anywhere to go. Nobody would want to immigrate to a victorious Germany. And in the whole history of the world no one has ever before heard of a victor from whose victory millions wish to escape. It is the world's most cosmic joke.

But what I must ask myself is: Why do any except actual Nazis fight for it?

My dear Hans:

I await with calm the communication that you have encouraged me to believe will reach me very soon, and am happy to learn of the others.

Meanwhile, we are holding all activities in abeyance. But it is obvious that whatever *we* do, certain things will not remain in abeyance. I read this week that Himmler has offered a two-million-marks reward for information about incendiarists who have set fire to Berlin apartment houses.

It is an odd item of news. The reward is unusually high, and so it is clear that major damage must have been done and that this activity is still going on. Also, it is not the Berlin police who offer the reward, but Himmler, the Chief of the Gestapo, who is seeking the culprits, from which we assume that political motives are recognized.

This is hardly the kind of activity in which a foreign agent would indulge. Burning apartment houses was not, for instance, in the program of the Nazi agents whom we have just arrested. They were after defense plants and rail-

road communications. Real incendiarists try to burn oil
tanks, or even food stores. Skilled saboteurs derail trains
by taking out bolts where the rails meet, or they plant
explosives in railroad yards, on bridges, and in armament
factories. I imagine such a trained saboteur would like to
set on fire police and Gestapo headquarters, in order to
destroy their files and dossiers. But he would certainly
not be interested in burning apartment houses. So we can
exclude the trained agents. It would not be worth their
while.

We know, of course, that German workers are very
hostile to this war, and especially to the Russian war, and
as a matter of fact we know that this week, in one port
town, dock workers smashed provision stores and fought a
Gestapo detachment sent to restore order. But they *did*
attack provision stores and not apartment houses — and
there is a great difference. Workers are very practical men
and know what they are doing. Their former Marxian
education taught them never to indulge in isolated activities that cannot be developed into real rebellion. So the
worker who is fighting Hitler and his war inside Germany
has other means of damaging the Nazi war machinery.
First, he works slowly and is sick as many days as possible.
He knows also that a handful of sand in the wheels of a
machine is more effective than a fire in an apartment house;
that nobody can find out whose fault it is if work on an
assembly belt is held up for hours because a wire is broken.
Or if he is a railway worker, he knows how difficult it is
to trace the responsibility if the posters on cars are changed
around so that those destined for Russia go to western

Germany and vice versa. Any man can make a mistake, and not even the Gestapo can read his mind. All sorts of industrial accidents can happen, and inasmuch as both factory and railroad material in Germany is badly worn anyhow, the fault may lie with the material, and there is no proof of sabotage. Workers have plenty of opportunity for sabotage where they are, and they do not go out and risk their lives burning up apartment houses.

So who did set fire to the Berlin apartment houses, Hans? I am not interested in collecting Mr. Himmler's two-million-marks reward. The two million marks are just so much paper anyhow. Still, I can tell him who burnt up the apartment houses, although he is going to have a very hard time finding them. And if he finds one or two it will not do any good, for they are not important as individuals. They are people in whom a spirit is exploding; their outbreaks are outbreaks of that spirit; and it is a contagious spirit — a spirit of despair and rebellion — any kind of rebellion — even senseless rebellion — against a world that is senseless. It is the spirit in a man that cries: 'It cannot go on like this; something must happen; I am fed up to the eyes; I have got to do something — and I cannot wait for anybody else to organize it for me.'

You, Hans, would not act in a way so planless. But your slowness can result in this: that matters are taken out of your hands, out of your control — indeed, out of any control.

You see, Hitler understands about the contagion of revolution. In his plans, the *Nazi* revolution was going to be contagious — it would be spread ahead of his troops, and with his troops, and do half his conquering for him. But that was his mistake, as any simple person could have told him, because nobody becomes a Nazi in order to be conquered. On the contrary, his troops have released another revolution — the revolution for liberty; the revolution against slavery; the revolution against senselessness and slaughter; the revolution against sapheads tricked out in an arrogant authority which has no inner basis.

And so, even while your troops are advancing, there is an inner spiritual turning of the tide. Something eventually happens in men who are sent out to do what is senseless and evil. Their hearts break, Hans. In the midst of a victory they are filled with inner despair, remorse, and anxiety. And in this despair, remorse, and anxiety they encounter their true comrades, namely, the people they are conquering, and they encounter the spirit of resistance of those people, and it is *that* revolutionary spirit which is now contagious all over Europe.

This revolutionary spirit is as enchained in Germany as it is in the conquered countries. It is held down by the same methods. But it also finds the same weapons. Does Mr. Himmler not know that he is sending his troops into *training* centers — sending them where they will learn how to *fight* Naziism? What is the burning of Berlin apartment houses? It is the scorched-earth policy which Germans have learned in Russia and Jugoslavia. Mr. Himmler is now offering a reward of two million marks to find guerrillas — in the heart of Berlin. Why does the Russian civilian burn down his own house — the roof over his head and his asylum? He knows perfectly well that it is against his immediate personal interest, but he would rather be homeless than provide homes for Nazis. And what else can be the idea of the Berlin incendiarists?

Hans, the human body and the human soul can stand only a certain amount. That certain amount is long since passed in the occupied countries, where the spirit cries, '*Anything* is better than this!' But that spirit crosses borders no matter how many guards you have on them, and whispers into *every* ear, 'Anything is better than this!' And a point is reached where nobody calculates any longer about such questions as 'What are the chances of this war? Who is likely to win?' There is only one cry: 'This cannot go on any longer! How can we stop it?'

For what good is it to take Rostov, when those who take it know in their innermost hearts and intelligences that they can do nothing with it after they have it — except to go on from there to some other place? What future can they see except a German population forever far from home, lost in a vast ocean of hostility? There comes a point when the issue is not who is winning, but the *war itself;* when political considerations are entertained only by those whose vested interest it is to entertain them. The masses of the people are united. The soldier at the front does not ask, 'Did we advance today?' He says, 'I want to go home.' The mother and wife do not say, 'Did my son or my husband reach Novocherkask?' They ask, 'When will he come home — and will he ever come home?'

So the fires are set alight to call attention to a spirit — to a spirit that finds only *this* way to send out a signal, since the spirit dare not speak.

I would say to Himmler: 'You can do nothing about this. You are looking in the wrong direction. You are looking for individuals who are incendiarists. You hope to arrest Herr Schmidt or Herr Mueller. But you must arrest an atmosphere — you must arrest the smoke and the flame itself.'

Who is responsible for the atmosphere? There was going to be no such atmosphere in this war. The German people were going to be psychologically conditioned not to create such an atmosphere. That was Doctor Goebbels's job. Will you arrest him now, because he failed? Shoot him? Then I could claim the two million marks. But, oddly enough, I shall plead the case of Doctor Goebbels. Shooting him will do no good. It did not help your food situation to replace Darré by Backe, and it will not do any good to replace Goebbels by Rosenberg, or some unknown dark horse, for there are forces let loose that are stronger than any person. These forces cry for peace and for a reasonable world; and if they do not get it they will set fires that will destroy your whole world.

All this you and I have known from the beginning. We wanted to save our world. We knew that a long and expanded war would bring only chaos. Hans, you must control the chaos; it cannot be controlled by those responsible for it — those who have created it. You cannot quench the spirit which creates the chaos — the spirit of revolt, but you must canalize it. Every symptom shows a revolutionary situation in Germany. If individuals and masses begin to act as they are doing, it is high time for responsible personalities to take over leadership, establish real aims, reach out to the world, and prevent your country from falling out of regimented anarchy, which Naziism is, into open anarchy, from which it can only be rescued by our troops.

Auf Wiederhören.

August 7, 1942

Dear Hans:

We certainly live in a fantastic world. You ask me to call the attention of the German people to a certain condition of affairs in Poland. You send me material, with the request that I rebroadcast it from here to the German people. Your motives lie outside the war itself; you try through me to make an appeal to German civilization, to right something monstrous. You appeal to me because you have no way of publishing the facts inside Germany.

I deduce that others of your group have attempted to reach people in England, for almost simultaneously with your report, which reached me by the usual channels, I received a somewhat similar report from Great Britain, though with fewer details.

Hans, I will fulfill your request. In the name of a great German, living inside Germany, I appeal to the German people to listen to the following facts and draw their own conclusions.

The Nazi Party has set up in Poland a human stud farm, in which it is using Polish girls and German boys, and Ger-

man girls and Polish boys, as mares and stallions. It is
called 'a camp for racial improvement' and it is located at
Hellenowa. Its purpose is to create a new racial Nordic
type for leadership of German-Polish populations through
enforced sexual intercourse between boys and girls who have
literally been kidnapped into this camp. I shall not mince
words, but say exactly what is happening.

A great modern camp has been laid out at Hellenowa.
It has playing-fields, swimming-pools, classrooms, hostels,
and small cabins each able to accommodate two persons.
It was built last autumn. As soon as it was finished, several
scores of German girls between the ages of fifteen and
eighteen, all of them exceptionally healthy and pretty, were
imported and housed in this camp. At the same time, in
the Lodz and Poznan districts, boys with blue eyes, blond
hair, and fine physiques began disappearing in a mysteri-
ous manner.

What happened to them was traced through the fact that
some of them were afterward rejected and sent home. Although counseled to secrecy, they told the facts. These boys
were first given a thorough medical examination in Lodz
and only those in a perfect state of health were retained.
These who were kept were given injections against gonor-
rhea and syphilis and sent to Hellenowa. There the youths
were sorted into couples: a Polish boy was assigned to every
German girl, and they were compelled to cohabit in the
cabins set up for that purpose.

In this camp, the youths follow a strict physical régime,
and no expense is spared to make their physical life splendid. At six o'clock they have reveille, tidy their huts, per-

form gymnastic exercises, and bathe. At seven they break-
fast, preferably in the open air. Next come two hours'
instruction in German, physics, nature study, and math-
ematics. Then they have games and military exercises,
stopping for luncheon, tea, and dinner. The food is ex-
cellent — better than any available to any German soldier or civilian. They have meat, milk, and fresh fruit
every day, with large quantities of white bread and fresh
vegetables. They live in conditions enjoyed by no class
or group in the whole of Europe. But they have one in-
escapable duty: each couple must have regular sexual intercourse, and this is supervised by the camp doctor.

This camp has been enlarged recently, during this summer. German boys have been brought in to service Polish
girls, abducted, like the Polish boys, from their parents.
There are now five hundred of them in camp. Several
Polish girls attempted suicide, in sheer horror at this enforced mating. But a very clever system of education, plus
their youthful blood, seeks to convince them that they are to
become, in this way, a future élite.

All pregnant Polish girls are sent immediately to Germany, where they must remain for good. The moment
their children are born, their rôle is ended. They are then
turned loose to work on the land or inhabit brothels. The
child is brought up by the state as a future leader. The
boys are returned to their families.

Women of Germany! Your children — the very best of
them — the physical pick of them — are being systematically brutalized. This camp is an experiment. So far only
a few hundred boys and girls are affected. But it is a camp

which thoroughly carries out a Nazi theory, and if the Nazis ever have the power, it will be universalized.

German boys and Polish boys are systematically taught to mistreat women. They are thrown together with beautiful girls under ideal physical conditions. Both boys and girls are virgin. They are not allowed to pick their first mates; they are picked for each other; but in the innocence of a first sexual experience they often come to love each other. No sooner is the mating consummated, however, than they are separated. Neither of them may ever see their baby, and the mother of that boy's first child is then thrown out as refuse upon society. He may not protect her; he may not protest; he must connive at the degradation of the mother of his child.

I warn you, women of Germany! Ruin is going to come upon you: ruin worse than defeat; ruin worse than a lost war. There will be no real marriage for any of you in the future Reich unless we defeat Hitler.

German girls! Hitler has told you that you are going to be the mothers of the future great German race. He has lied to you. The future mothers of leaders are not going to be German girls even chiefly, but Polish girls, Czech girls, Russian, French, and Norwegian girls — any girl that fulfills certain physical specifications of Nordic beauty. You poor fools; you are letting your sons die in order to conquer concubines for your men! And you poor concubines, German and otherwise, who are fed and fatted merely as brood mares — to be thrown into harness when the function is performed!

Your men are being spoiled forever for normal life with

normal women under normal conditions. Your men have been away for years now in occupied countries. The Nazi Party has introduced another institution, that of honorary wives, and your husband, my dear woman, has now got another wife — in France, or Norway, or wherever he may be. And do you think that he is going to remember you while he is in her arms — or that she is going to encourage him to remember you?

Nothing is too good for a German soldier, says the Nazi Party. In all the occupied countries houses of prostitution have been opened. The inhabitants are not women whose career is prostitution — stupid and used up. They are the prettiest and best-bred women, whom the German army has forced into brothels. They are young — some of them are only fifteen years old. And while you sit under bombs and starve, your husbands are being offered these specially selected tidbits of girls. Do you think you will be able to make life interesting for him when he comes home to family cares?

Are you a young German girl engaged to a German pilot? Then I can tell you that the German pilots graduating from the training school at Swidnik Air Field in Poland have just had a whole bevy of girls, rounded up by the Gestapo, presented to them as a gift.

Hans, you have asked me to tell this and much more to the German people. I will: but on another occasion. Before I finish this message, there are some things I want to say to *you*.

You want me to tell this to the German people who may still think that Hitler is waging this war for the glory of the

German people. But by looting Europe he is dissolving the German race. He is creating the greatest race mixture on earth. My concern is not the German race. My concern is the future — the coming back to normal times; and the longer this war goes on, the more impossible that will be. Every institution of life is being destroyed, and above all, the home. For Danzig — over which you started the war — you disintegrate Germany. That you also disintegrate all Europe is beside the point. What good do you get out of it? Do you want to butter your bitter bread with *Schadenfreude?* [1]

The question of who wins or loses this war is becoming increasingly irrelevant for Germany. You have lost the war already — lost it in the midst of your conquests — because you have lost yourselves. How do you conceivably think that this régime can establish peace in Europe? Do you think that there can ever be peace with the fathers and mothers of girls who have been treated like this?

Hans, you have sent me this information for one single purpose: you want me to help you stop this by revealing the facts to the German people. But if you think you can cure a mental disease by stopping one thing like this, you are wrong. The raping of girls is a political question, and a more important political question than frontiers. You take a certain responsibility in helping to get these facts known. But you have to take a greater responsibility: you have to cure a mental disease and get rid of these perverted monsters who govern your once great country. Otherwise ruin will come over Germany in a form that you cannot possibly

[1] Malicious enjoyment of others' misfortunes.

foresee. It will not even come from us. It will come from the terrible sickness of the soul that is already corroding the whole of German life. That is your defeat. And the sirocco of your defeat is blowing over Germany like a pestilential wind. God help you, Hans.

Dear Hans:

Your last letter reached me just as I was about to write to you. The picture you give of Europe is appalling; it is heartbreaking. But the picture that you give of your own state of mind is what really perturbs me, for I see that you, a man so much under his own control, with an inner freedom so deep and natural, are yourself a victim of everything about you. Despair is eating away your will and eating away your faith. I wish I could speak directly to that despair and reawaken that faith; for without it, you and all Europe are lost — lost beyond anything that we can do for you now, or tomorrow, or in the future.

You realize now what you should have realized from the beginning — that there is no fate for Germany apart from the fate of Europe, and that every wound in the body of Europe is a wound in the body of Germany. You say, 'Europe is being bled so white that even new infusions of blood cannot save her.' You say, 'Things can be camouflaged for a little while longer, but not so long as America seems to think.' You speak of the sickness of the heart and mind that has become epidemic, and that you fear will make any reconstruction impossible, no matter whose may be the victory. 'We have conquered,' you cry, 'only to be tied to a sinking ship — the sinking ship of our own conquests.'

Hans, today I speak to bring you comfort. The war will not end as you think it will. You see things from far too short a perspective and from far too narrow a room. You are right in your cry against our lack of preparedness, against our too delayed recognition of our duty to intervene, and to intervene long ago. You fear that our delay will bring us too late — before we bring liberation and succor the body of Europe will be dead. From every word of your letter I can see that you are convinced that Europe is a lost continent.

Dying in Russia, starving to death everywhere, rioting in the Balkans, Germany herself, bitter and grim, marching senselessly God knows where; every mouthful of bread eaten in hatred under the envious eyes of the neighbor, all courtesy departed from life — all the gestures of kindness that mitigate the lot of man on this earth — and the greatest of all curses: helplessness before the question, What is it all for?

Yes, that Europe you correctly describe. You see a continent sinking in the morass of doom.

I am so impressed with your picture that I seem to myself to be almost tactless and brutal when I must reaffirm to you my absolute faith in the future — faith in a future for Europe, for Germany, and for the whole world. My intelligence tells me that your picture of things as they are at this moment is a correct picture. But the shock of it is not so strong, because all this we could both of us see in advance. We saw it, if I must remind you, when we last met on the very verge of the outbreak of war.

But you, Hans, have been calculating. Not trusting your positive inner knowledge, the intuition of your senses, and the admonitions of your conscience, you have been calculating that it might possibly turn out differently for the Nazis. Your last letter is an immense change from those which I have had previously; and I can see with perfect clarity that your despair today arises from the fact that you do not act, and that you are the victim and prisoner of your own previous actions.

What did you do? You watched the rise of Naziism with revulsion and horror. *You* were pure; *you* would have nothing to do with this beastly apparition. You fled from it — and where did you fly? When Hitler came to power, some of your friends left Germany. They emigrated. You would not emigrate; Germany was your country; and for that I had great respect. But you wanted to escape — and so you emigrated, too. You thought there was one place where you could remain pure — and to that place you emigrated. That was the German Reichswehr. You thought: The soldier is beyond politics and beyond corruption. He belongs to a sort of holy order of obedience, devotion, and discipline. You put on the uniform of the Reichswehr as a monk puts on his cassock, and in that gesture sought to renounce all the evils of your world.

But you are captured in your monastery. Its walls were already violated long before you entered it. The traditions of honor and chivalry of the German Reichswehr could not exist in the sort of state of which it was the instrument. It was an instrument of Germany and Germany was Hitler; and it has fought, not its war, but Hitler's war.

How could you have failed to realize this from the beginning? You should have seen it in logic. You should have seen it on the night of June 30, 1934 — when there was not a victory for the Reichswehr but a compromise. You should have seen it when Hindenburg died and his army was unable to reveal the falsification of his testament. You should have seen it in February, 1938, when General von Fritsch and thirteen other generals were dismissed. You had hoped, out of the Reichswehr, to create an instrument that would reform and purify the Nazi state; but you have helped to create a *Knechtschaft* (body of mercenaries) for the Hitler state.

Therefore its guilt is upon you, and that consciousness of guilt is paralyzing you. And you see that the hatred against the Nazi state includes you; and you cry aloud to the world, 'We were pure' — but nobody listens and nobody believes.

You went into the Reichswehr because you would take no part in the subjugation of your own people. You stood aside from the excesses of the S.A. and the S.S. You said, 'This guilt shall not be upon me.' Like Pontius Pilate, you washed your hands of the blood of just men, while the organized mob cried that Barabbas be released. You protected some Jews; you helped some Socialists to escape.

It was hopeless, Hans. Today young Germans under your command stumble and fall dead on the soil of a country that they love — Russia. *You* drive them farther and farther into limbo. Under *your* orders, populations are slaughtered from Oslo to Rostov Under *your* orders, innocent hostages are shot. Under *your* orders, trainloads of helpless Jews are transported to the Polish swamps, there to perish. Under *your* orders, young men whose only crime is love and loyalty to their own motherlands are ruthlessly executed.

You thought it was a drastic step when you got in contact with me and asked for help. That would have been a drastic step if you had broken once and for all with this evil and already shipwrecked thing. And now I tell you, you cannot be saved by the Reichswehr. You can only be saved by yourself, and in company with all the selves that feel as you do. What you say in your camps and to each other, you must say aloud, and to the world.

You ask me, 'What must we do?' The first thing you must do is a personal and spiritual thing: you must recover your *inner* freedom, and out of it find the strength to recover your outer freedom. It is amazing to me that a man who has never feared death, but has always looked it calmly and quietly in the eye, will risk it for a cause that he despises and in which he sees no ray of hope and nothing but despair, and will not risk it for the faith of his heart and the conviction of his intelligence.

What you risk your life for, Hans, determines whether you are full of hope or eaten away with despair. And that is true for an individual, it is true for a nation, and it is true for the whole world.

I am full of optimism. America is full of optimism. We are realists We know the task we have to do — and how

terrible a task it is. We know that we are not doing it as
well as we should; and we know that we shall have to
pay for our negligence, and our selfishness, and our self-
satisfaction.

Yet our war is cleansing us of a feeling of guilt. It is not
loading us with one. We see with clarity the kind of world
we want to live in, and the kind of world we *can* live in, and
the kind of world we *intend* to live in — and it makes us
happy, because we know it is the kind of world *everybody*
wants to live in.

If we intended to conquer; if we intended to steal; if we
intended to crush this civilization or that, destroy this nation
or that, in order that our own might somehow be fertilized
by the manure of what we had destroyed — then we, too,
should be in despair. But we go to liberate, and therefore
we fight with laughter.

We as a nation are not so greatly talented — not more
talented than you. We are not so pure — we share all the
vices of mankind. But it is the best of us that goes into this
war — not the worst of us. It is the best in our motives
that impels us — and not the worst. It is the most generous
of our instincts that drives us — and not the most mean.
We are not governed by the scum of America — as Germany is governed by the scum of Germany. If we spill
blood, it will not be spilled by hands systematically trained
in spilling the blood of their brothers. We have no Goering
in our army with von Schleicher's blood upon his hands.

Hans, believe me, Germany can be just as happy as
America. There is no geographic reason for your despair;
no racial reason; I am sure Germany could be as happy in

a European federation of free and equal states as Wisconsin, or New York, or Kansas is happy in *our* great brotherhood.

But you cannot become happy by destroying the only prospect and basis for your happiness. *You cannot be happy unless you are loved.* You know that I, in Vermont, should not be better off by subjugating New Hampshire. I live happily because I live in a great brotherhood. I live happily because no one *fears* me — and so I need fear no one.

And we will win the war, because we are not afraid of our victory. We will be loved for our victory, and therefore we shall have it.

Cheer up, Hans. The world is not coming to an end. It is about to begin a new life!

My dear Hans:

When we last sat together and discussed the world, before this terrible war began, we agreed — do you remember? — that the present anarchy could not go on, and that the twentieth century must see a synthesis emerge between the political principles of American democratic freedom, the socialist ideas of Russia, the world-wide sense and statesmanship of Britain, and the great organizational power of Germany.

You must have observed that, despite all the setbacks and confusions, such a world is emerging — alas, against Germany instead of with her.

I speak of this because of your continuous desire to discuss peace. But you cannot discuss peace from an isolated German viewpoint — any more than I can discuss it from an isolated American viewpoint. There is no sense in asking what concessions will the world make to Germany — in regard to boundaries and spheres of influence and so forth. The answer to that question is, 'Every concession and absolute equality, provided that we can agree upon the kind of world we wish to live in.'

There has been much talk over here about the re-education of the German people after this war, and about the disarmament of aggressors. But it becomes increasingly clear that the problem is not only of the re-education of Germany and Japan, but of the re-education of the peoples of the world. The great intellectual shock of our times, Hans, and the one to which no people as a whole has as yet adjusted itself, is the shock of discovering the world for the first time. By that I mean discovering that we are, in the most intimate sense, as nations and cultures, and as members of nations and cultures, inextricably tied together throughout this globe.

And as for the disarmament of aggressors — every people must be clamoring for disarmament after this war, for if victory merely means that some victorious group must bear this intolerable burden, then everyone is going to lose the war. I am sure the desire of all peoples, including the German, after this war will be to rebuild what has been destroyed, and to put all our energies into turning this suffering and impoverished earth into a prosperous organized world.

So let us speak of the real issues, not in a Utopian way, as we all have done in former times, but theoretically and realistically — in a manner that an ordinary politician can understand.

You have heard of the visits of Churchill to Roosevelt, of Molotoff to Churchill and then to Roosevelt, and now of Churchill to Stalin; and naturally there are speculations as to the military significance of these visits. They do, of course, have military significance. Of that I shall not speak, nor should I be allowed to. The military significance of the visits will be revealed by action. But they also have a very great political significance, for it must be clear to you that no military coalition of this sort could be accomplished without far-reaching political agreements.

The same holds true on the Axis side. As I have pointed out before, this war that you have been forced to fight by the political mismanagement of your country is neither Hitler's war, nor a Reichswehr war — Haushofer's war, for instance. On that matter you can consult the documentary evidence, in Hitler's *Mein Kampf*, in his speeches, and in your own military literature, particularly that emanating from the Munich school of geo-politics.

Hitler wished to fight Russia in alliance with the British Empire, which he greatly admired. Haushofer wished to fight the British Empire, which he considered ripe for collapse, in alliance with Russia. And actually, your political leadership has attempted to carry out each of these programs. Hitler offered the alliance to Great Britain at various times, and even as late as on September 1, 1939, immediately before he attacked Poland, and again when he sent Hess to England in May, 1941.

But in the meantime he also tried Haushofer's project, and in November, 1940, when Molotoff was in Berlin, Hitler offered an all-out alliance to the Soviet Union. All the talk about the holy crusade against communism is sheer bosh, because Hitler *wanted* an alliance with Stalin, and the history of our times, when it is objectively written, will prove it.

From a military point of view, there were obvious advantages for Germany in such an alliance, and there were also obvious advantages for the others. Great Britain could have preserved her empire, and even have enlarged it. Hitler would have made Britain no trouble in India. On the contrary, he would have been glad to aid Britain in the ruthless suppression of nationalist movements in India. His feeling toward Indian national aspirations is made perfectly clear in *Mein Kampf*.

The same is true for the Haushofer concept that Hitler tried to follow late in 1940. The Soviet Union could have been preserved intact, and could even have been enlarged, since Haushofer was prepared to grant Persia, a large part of China, and India as special spheres of influence to the Soviets.

Now, if these alliances which Hitler offered were superficially, at least, of advantage to either Britain or Russia, why was it not possible to realize them? And why, on the other side, can we make our coalition? Superficially a coalition between Britain, Russia, the United States, and China seems fantastic.

Believe me, Hans, the accomplishment of this coalition is not due primarily to military reasons, but to political reasons. Our worlds that seem so different — the British world, the American, the Chinese, and the Russian — *are* able to approach each other, and will create together something new and something world-wide. But the Axis world could not do that with any country that was not Fascist — I include Japan among the Fascists — or that was not prepared to commit suicide. I said the Axis world; I did not say *Germany*. It is absolutely clear that Germany could fit into the pattern of such a new world. Indeed, much of the inspiration for such a world has come from German scholars and thinkers for the last forty years. At any rate, step by step, the pattern of the future world is beginning to emerge, as the result of persistent and sincere attempts to find an agreement satisfactory to Britain, America, Russia, and China.

You must not think that this will be a future four-power world. The smaller nations are in it, not overruled, but contributing ideas and proposals. It is our earnest intention to include a Free France, and there is room in it for such a great power as Germany, provided it is a Germany which accepts the principles of freedom and equality.

What Germany has to fear is what Japan is inflaming in the Far East — namely, an intense hatred against the whole of western civilization. Japanese publicists now, even in the face of their alliance with Germany and Italy, are openly preaching the extermination of all white men in the Far East. They even dare to say openly that they will eventually have a showdown with Germany in case of an Axis victory. The alliance with Japan is ideologically correct, because Japan shares all the major Nazi views. Yet it is catastrophic for inner reasons; for the logic of fascism is that having consumed all other states and nations, the survivors must attempt to consume each other.

So, when I go on beseeching you, Hans, to set about forming a Germany which can join the new world that is in birth, I suggest the only possibility for Germany. The alternatives are a complete victory for us with a Germany encircled and isolated, or the final alternative, an endless war that will destroy the whole earth in an apocalypse of madness.

As you know, I believe completely in our victory, but obviously I should prefer to win it not merely by military force and long-continued destruction, but by universal enlightenment — by a universal act of conversion.

The people everywhere know that what I am saying is right. In our world the people push our leaders in this direction every day; and in your world those who do not join the people will soon have reason to be afraid of them. I have told you before: You can make wars against nations, even successful wars, but you cannot make war against the human race. Your poet Schiller said of the human race: 'It is greater than you esteem it. It will break its bonds.' I say, 'It will create the world it wants; and that is not a Nazi world.'

August 28, 1942

Dear Hans:

Perhaps you know what has just happened in France.
Pierre Laval went to the German authorities begging that
more food should be left in France for the hungering population. He was told that the Nazi Government might consider increasing the rations, provided that the French Government got rid of the foreigners and Jews living in France.
As a result, Laval has agreed to deport sixteen thousand
people from the occupied zone and ten thousand from the
unoccupied. They go to an unknown destination in eastern
Europe. It is a pure and simple death sentence. Families
with children over five from the occupied zone, and over
two from the unoccupied zone, may take their children with
them. Children under five or two are simply to become
orphans. One thousand have been taken from the camp
at Gurs, seven hundred from Vernet, seven hundred from
Les Milles. Men, women, and children are being arrested
in the streets of Marseilles, Toulouse, and Lyons to make
up the quota.

What can the outside world say to this? Can we say

it has not been done by *Germany?* Can I say I know
one *man* in Germany who is not like this? And if I am
asked what is he doing against it, shall I merely reply that
he is communicating occasionally with me? You know,
and even the members of your Government know, that
I was one of the independent people in this world who
after the last war protested with my voice and pen against
many of the provisions of the Treaty of Versailles. What
shall I think now of my own attitude? Was Clemenceau
after all right, who said that the German people were a race
of barbarians? Before the whole civilized world present-
day Germany appears as a Herod slaughtering the innocents. Day by day Hitler dips the hands of Germany in new
blood.

To his crimes he now adds infanticide, and he adds it in
the name of the German people.

Hans, I appeal to your religion, to your conscience, to
your German sense of honor and decency! It belonged
once to the principles of German military honor never to
trample upon a beaten enemy. These men, women, and
children, who once fled to France, and are now being
dumped into some wilderness in the east, there to starve,
after their infant children have been torn from their arms,
were defeated long ago. They could no longer make any
contribution one way or another to the war. Even the
French, in their desperation, left them in peace. Hundreds
of them fled into Switzerland, and even the Swiss — yes,
Hans, the German Swiss — pressed as they are by the
Nazis, and without adequate food and coal for themselves,
have not the heart to deliver these people over to Hitler.

How can a German from the Third Reich look a Swiss German in the eye today? What has been done has been to tell a starving French mother, 'I will give your child food, if you will kill a foreign child.'

If there is a God in heaven, the punishment for this will be terrible.

But, Hans, let us think coldly: Why is it done?

One motive is petty revenge. Miserable little officials who have escaped dying on the eastern front add their killing job to the terrible scene. To war they add massacre.

But Hitler has another purpose. Can you not see that he is systematically trying to create in the world such a hatred of and contempt for the whole German race that the German people do not *dare* to stop the war? Goebbels has been saying it over and over again: 'We must win; otherwise the revenge will be terrifying.'

The Nazi Government knows that the world does not look for revenge, but for reorganization. Hitler fears the decency of the rest of the world. Therefore, he seeks to engender in the world such a hatred and fury that its decency cannot be a weapon. He wants to be able to say truthfully, 'Either victory with me or extinction!'

That policy is very dangerous for the German people. One cannot say that it will not be at least partially successful unless you act before it is too late.

We are not living in a world of saints, but of human beings. Theoretically we know that the German people must be reintegrated into a world that makes sense. Theoretically we know that Frau Schmidt of Dessau is not responsible for this. Yet this could not happen in my country, without thousands of people risking their lives to cry, 'Stop it!' I know the faults of my country, but I also know that I would not sit by and see my country do this; no, I would not, not if it meant prison or death, or death with torture. I would not be a party to this. And I should not be alone, either. Where are *you*, Hans?

I understand it less, inasmuch as you have nothing to lose. What is your choice? Millions of Germans are dying anyhow. Why? To fasten upon your necks forever this unspeakable régime, and to fasten it upon the necks of the world?

In the same moment when my private information tells me of this unspeakable crime committed in France, the open prints tell me of Hitler's latest crime against the German people. We learn that the former Minister of Justice, a *Deutsch-Nationaler* named Doctor Franz Guertner, has died. He was not a great character, God knows; but nevertheless he had inherited an old tradition of former times. His successor is Doctor Otto Thierack, the former President of the People's Court and one of the leading henchmen of the Nazi Party. This man has sentenced thousands to death for doing nothing more than disagree with the crimes of the Nazi Party. Why has he been promoted from a job that he so excellently fulfilled for Hitler? Because he has had experience with one people's court, and from now on every court in Germany is going to be a people's court.

The decree announcing his appointment empowers him to provide for 'a forceful administration of justice,' in order that 'the problems confronting the great German Reich may be fulfilled.' He is told to establish a National Socialist administration throughout all the courts of Germany, and he is given the right to suspend all the existing laws in Germany. At the same time, there is a complete shakeup in the whole judiciary administration of Germany — all in the same direction.

I warned you months ago what was coming, when the duly acquired rights were abolished. Do you remember when that happened? It happened at the same time when Hitler himself had to admit the terrible German defeat in the Russian winter campaign. Hitler was afraid then of losing control inside Germany, and so tightened his hold over the courts. Even that was not enough: nothing can be enough. Pressure can always be increased, and even this will not be the last step. Hitler is going to take you into another winter campaign. He is clairvoyant about this coming campaign, so this time he fortifies himself against the wrath of the German people in advance. He is already collecting clothing for the coming winter — this time in August, instead of December — and he is rigging the courts to massacre malcontents.

I understand his position, Hans, and his mentality, but I do not understand yours. I do not know why you wait and hope, in the face of absolutely certain collapse and chaos.

Do you think that the wretchedness of the slaughter of the innocents in France offsets the wretchedness of the judicial slaughters about to begin in Germany? Do you not see the accumulation of an agony which will blow up the world? Do you not see that what a high German officer, in a neutral country, told me in the spring of 1940 is true? I met him at the house of a friend, where he was on furlough. He had no idea who I was, or that I spoke German. And he said to his hostess, 'Madam, my country is in the hands of the worst crowd of criminals who ever governed a great people.'

Do you expect to win a war when you cannot even govern yourselves, my dear Hans?

The handwriting is written on the wall, my friend. Behind governments, beyond governments, believe me, the whole world is rising. The gorge is in every throat; disgust and indignation in every heart. It is useless to live, if this lives.

Dear Hans:

This week begins the fourth year of Hitler's war. How little any German thought that it would last this long! How many promises have been made to the German people about the length of this war! First, there was going to be no war at all, and all would be bloodless victories. Then it was to be over in 1939 after the defeat of Poland; then in 1940; then in 1941.

Now I see that when Hitler opened the Winter Help campaign, on the thirty-first of August — the last day of the third war year — he made no further promises at all.

I only see that he again repeats, as though it were an obsession with him, that Britain and America attacked Germany. 'If today British and American agents assert that they desire a new and better world system, why was it necessary for them to attack Germany?' That is what Hitler said.

The German people know that this is a gigantic lie. Their memories are certainly not so short but that they can remember the origins of this war. Certainly they can remember that in the months before it began, every conceivable concession was made to Hitler. Certainly they can remember that the world stood by, that France broke her treaty with Russia and Czechoslovakia, that the Government of Britain persuaded the Czechs peacefully to relinquish the Sudetenland — all in the interests of peace; and that the reward for this was a Nazi invasion of Prague, in contradiction of Hitler's solemnly given promises. Certainly they can remember that the first soldier to cross a border and open attack was a German soldier, and that the attack occurred on Polish soil!

Britain, Hans, has never broken a treaty, and surely the German people know that Hitler was aware of the existing treaties. So of what use is the formal statement that Britain and France declared war without being attacked? The invasion of Poland was an attack on Britain under the existing treaties, solemnly and publicly reaffirmed on the eve of the attack. Even after the attack occurred, there were two full days in which the Polish Ambassador Lipski held himself in readiness to reopen negotiations, while the British Government waited and warned. Only on the third of September, when the German armies were devastating everything before them, did the two western powers acknowledge their obligations and declare that a state of war existed.

Incidentally, Hans, almost the same formula was used by Hitler in declaring war on the United States after we had been dealt a lightning blow by Japan, without any previous declaration of war. Hitler made war; we eventually acknowledged it.

I am interested that Hitler is now apologizing for this war. In all the years in which he built up the Nazi War Party, he never thought that war for *Lebensraum* needed an apology. On the contrary, he said that the sword must conquer the soil for the plow, and that no alliances are any good except as their purpose is war. And if one sets out to conquer *Lebensraum* of unlimited extent, one must count on a little opposition to it. In the very same speech — August 31 — Hitler said, 'In this gigantic struggle German and allied Axis soldiers have in this year vastly extended the living space of the people of Europe.' Now, Hans, you cannot have Germany just defending herself, and extending her living space at the same time. Or have the German people ceased to have an interest in the logicalness of Mr. Hitler's remarks?

But leave this discussion aside. The British and American 'agents,' as Mr. Hitler called us in his speech, do indeed intend to make a new and better world system, and we welcome to our fellowship all men and women of all countries, allies or officially enemies. We exclude from it the members of the Nazi Party, because we have seen the new and better world system that they are trying to make, and we spit on it.

Whose agent am I? Yours, Hans — and working overtime because you are still too afraid.

Does Hitler honestly think that the 'new and better world system' is the kind of régime that Quisling has set up in Norway, or Alfred Rosenberg is scheming for occupied Russia, or Hacha is trying to run in Czechoslovakia, or the one that is raging in Poland? Ha! Let Hitler ask the

youth of the world what they think of it! Let him ask
American youth! What an awakening he is due for — and
not at too distant a date!

Hitler's speech, nevertheless, cheered me up enormously.
Why is he afraid of talk about a new and better world
system? Because the people of Germany want it as much
as we want it! You do not need to tell me that the German
people are horrified at this new shipment of forty thousand refugees from France to the east. They know as well
as we do that it is not only basely cruel but profoundly
senseless. I hope they see, however, that the Nazi Party
is using the already inadequate European transportation
system for such a preposterous purpose, and is hastening
your defeat out of the fear that the party might otherwise be
defeated.

The whole speech is a very feeble preface to the beginning
of the fourth year of the Nazi war. I know how ominous
are the words 'fourth year.' More ominous than they were
last time, because the German casualties of the first three
years of this war are already greater than the sum of the
whole four years of the last war.

And the casualties that are ahead — I shudder when I
contemplate them, for we know that the real war is just
beginning.

Is this clear to the German people, Hans? The first two
years were nothing. In 1939 and 1940 Germany knocked
out nothing but fundamentally weak powers. The strength
of France was overrated for years. Even in the last war
France was saved at the last minute by the intervention of
the United States, and she has never recovered from the

casualties of it. Britain only began her defensive war in the fall of 1940, and is only beginning to accomplish her preparations for a real offensive war now. She has lost practically nothing in either men or materials as yet.

The real war began when Hitler had the tremendous folly to attack Russia. You have been in a war against one major power for fourteen months, and I think that single war is enough for Germany. But, my friend, there are three major wars that still have to be fought, and they all have to be fought in a manner which makes it impossible for the German people to defend their own homeland; for while you pretend to conquer 'living space' a thousand miles away from the German border, and while your Fuehrer is beginning to have humane worries about India, all the military power of Germany is unable to prevent the devastation of that living space which is German soil, German history, German tradition, and the German people.

How have the Nazis defended Cologne, Mainz, Frankfurt, Düsseldorf, Duisburg, Münster, Osnabrück, Bremen, Hamburg, Rostock, Lübeck, Kiel, Nürnberg, Saarbrücken, Stuttgart, Königsberg, Stettin, and even Berlin and Munich — all of which the whole world admits belong to German living space? And how will you defend, this coming winter, all these and all the other German towns that have so far been spared?

You yourself admit, Hans, that it cannot be done. All that your High Command promises is reprisals — once you have finished with Russia.

The truth is that your country, in the fourth year of the war, begins a world war: a world war that cannot be won by blitzes, as Britain first proved, and Russia later proved. In the fourth year you have to begin a war of position and a war of attrition, and against whom? A still far from conquered Russia with great man-power reserves; a Britain that is just beginning to fight; an America so far untouched — with all the great reserves of Brazil added to it since I last spoke to you. Brazil has forty-four million inhabitants, or just as many people as you have conquered in Russia. Together the people fighting from this hemisphere alone add up to more than two hundred millions.

Hans, tell your people to go to the public libraries and look back over pre-war numbers of the *Militaerisches Wochenblatt*, and the *Deutsche Wehr*. Let them read the articles written there by Germany's greatest military minds. You will find that all of them said, over and over again, that Germany could not win a long war of attrition, but only short and limited wars of movement. That is why Hitler wants peace. He knows that whatever of usefulness to Germany can be conquered is already conquered, and that the last conquests in Russia have been far too costly.

That is just why he cannot get peace. Because we know it, too; the least child in the street knows it. And we have not gone through all our suffering to give anything to Hitler, the instigator of this bloody holocaust.

Hans, my dear friend: the first three years of the Nazi Blitz are over. Now our war begins. Pray that we, and our leaders, through all the sufferings ahead, may keep our aims clean. And I promise you that I will fight on, for a new and better world system.

THE END

Date Due

172	Mar 24		
8370	Dec 18		
8095	July 30		
7665	Feb 19		
7665	Mar 13		
8800	Mar 21		
MAR 2 6 '54			
APR 20 '56			
MAY 4 '56			
JAN 30			